Joseph Chamberlain, Radical and Imperialist

Harry Browne

LONGMAN

Longman
1724-1974

DA565
.C4 B76

LONGMAN GROUP LIMITED
London

Associated companies, branches and
representatives throughout the world

All rights reserved. No part of this
publication may be reproduced, stored in
a retrieval system, or transmitted in any form
or by any means, electronic, mechanical,
photocopying, recording, or otherwise,
without the prior permission of the
Copyright owner.

© Longman Group Ltd 1974

First published 1974
ISBN 0 582 35214 2
Printed in Great Britain by Whitstable Litho, Whitstable, Kent

Contents

Introduction to the Series

The seminar method of teaching is being used increasingly. It is a way of learning in smaller groups through discussion, designed both to get away from and to supplement the basic lecture techniques. To be successful, the members of a seminar must be informed — or else, in the unkind phrase of a cynic — it can be a 'pooling of ignorance'. The chapter in the textbook of English or European history by its nature cannot provide material in this depth, but at the same time the full academic work may be too long and perhaps too advanced.

For this reason we have invited practising teachers to contribute short studies on specialised aspects of British and European history with these special needs in mind. For this series the authors have been asked to provide, in addition to their basic analysis, a full selection of documentary material of all kinds and an up-to-date and comprehensive bibliography. Both these sections are referred to in the text, but it is hoped that they will prove to be valuable teaching and learning aids in themselves.

Note on the System of References:

A bold number in round brackets (5) in the text refers the reader to the corresponding entry in the Bibliography section at the end of the book.

A bold number in square brackets, preceded by 'doc' [docs 6, 8] refers the reader to the corresponding items in the section of Documents, which follows the main text.

PATRICK RICHARDSON
General Editor

Acknowledgements

We are grateful to the following for permission to reproduce copyright material: Cassell and Company Ltd and A.S. Barnes & Company, Inc. for extracts from *Joseph Chamberlain* by P. Fraser: Harvester Press Ltd for an extract from *The Radical Programme* 1971 by D.A. Hamer; Macmillan, London and Basingstoke for extracts from *Life of Joseph Chamberlain* by Julian Amery; and John Murray (Publishers) Ltd for an extract from *Life of C.S. Parnell 1899* by R.B. O'Brien.

The cover picture is reproduced by permission of the National Portrait Gallery.

PART ONE

Background

1 Birmingham in the 1860s

Unlike Athens, Paris or Florence, the name of Birmingham does not immediately stir the imagination, does not immediately conjure up a vision of splendid streets or of a great and glorious past. Yet for many Birmingham men in the late nineteenth century, the city stood for progress like its motto, Forward, and seemed for one intoxicating moment to be leading England, and therefore Europe and the world. Chamberlain's dream of creating a rival to the Champs Elysées in the newly planned townscape of the city still seems, even with the engineering triumphs of the 1960s, very far from realisation: the vision was there and Corporation Street is its slightly drab reality.

This city, lying at the centre of England and buttressed by the Black Country, was in the 1860s a growing, prosperous and stable community with an appendix of ancient trades in the central areas and comfortable suburbs beginning already to spread to Edgbaston and Handsworth. In the middle of the city the jewellery quarter and gunsmiths' shops still stood and some of the solider citizens, like Barrow, the grocer, still lived with well-established lawyers around Newhall Street. Nearby was a warren of squalid streets in St. Mary's Ward, where the very poor starved, quarrelled and got drunk. On the fringe of the city, industrial areas — Smethwick, Witton and Small Heath (stimulated after 1861 by the Birmingham Small Arms Company) - grew and expanded and the city pushed out its lines towards them. The real agent of social change was to be the tramway in the 1870s, and city streets crowded round the new tramlines. The railway line to fashionable Sutton was opened in 1862 and the country area around Gravelly Hill and beyond was now available for colonisation by city commuters (7).

Commercially and industrially Birmingham served the world, but it also served the local region, the Black Country. Joseph Chamberlain with his euphoric vision was to claim that Birmingham was under-shopped. Certainly the elegant iron and glass arcades of the 1870s and '80s were to provide, as they still do, magnificent and imaginative shopping centres; nevertheless even in the 1860s Birmingham acted as shopping magnet to all the small towns around, to Bilston and

Wolverhampton, to Wednesbury and Dudley. Socially and culturally, too, Birmingham with its great music centre in the Town Hall, its literary and philosophical life in the Midland Institute, its splendid nonconformist chapels with their intellectually formidable preachers, set standards which no small town could match. Part of the Birmingham mission was to equip the city with a rich civic life which would reflect its importance in the Midlands (9).

Birmingham's economic life was distinct and separate from that of the Black Country. If variety was the distinctive quality of Birmingham industry, nevertheless within that variety four main trades dominated the industrial life of the town: jewellery, brass goods, guns and buttons. Of these brass was clearly the most important, and one of the main staples of the city. A local industrialist, W.C. Aitken, wrote lyrically of its importance in the 1860s.

> What Manchester is in cotton [he wrote] Bradford in wool and Sheffield in steel, Birmingham is in brass; its articles of cabinet and general brassfoundry are to be found in every part of the world; its gas fittings in every city and town into which gas has been introduced, from Indus to the Poles - on the railways on every country and on every sea, its locomotive and marine engine solid brass tubes generate the vapour which impels the locomotive over the iron road, and propels the steam-boat over the ocean wave.

Around 8,000 Birmingham men worked in brass and only slightly fewer worked in the jewellery trade producing goods of almost every kind, table ware, wine measures, rings, diamond mountings. The gun trade had a labour force of 6,000 working in an industry which catered for the wealthy sportsman on the grouse moors as well as for a West African market needing cheap muskets. Roughly the same number worked producing the buttons for which Birmingham was famous, made of glass, papier maché, linen-covered, enamelled buttons in magnificent variety (8).

Slightly below these were other less important trades. From Birmingham came steel pens, almost a monopoly of the market. Iron beds, brass beds, wire and woodscrews were, with so much else, made there.

Black Country industry differed significantly. The local raw materials were iron and coal and consequently its manufacturers were mainly finished iron goods. There were, however, some light industries similar to those in Birmingham. Wolverhampton produced its own iron bedsteads, an industry subsidiary to its prime products: cutting tools such as scythes and spades. Glass was produced in Smethwick and Stourbridge; West Bromwich had its domestic hollow ware, scuttles, pans and kettles. Throughout the whole Black Country nailmaking still thrived, although even in this trade each small town often had its local specialism such as Halesowen's rivets. It was the two heavy industries of coal and iron which gave the region its particular character: slag heap and small town depended on these, and alongside these two giants were ancillary iron industries producing iron wheels, gas holders, iron tanks and galvanised sheets. Paradoxically it was in Birmingham in the 1860s that the first major threat to Black Country prosperity was being developed, for in Great Hampton Street Siemens was working out the open hearth system which was to revolutionise the making of steel and thereby to make archaic many Black Country iron products (9).

Structurally Birmingham industry depended still on the small unit of production, and in many trades the domestic system, or a combination of factory with domestic system, continued to hold its own. Of great economic importance within this system was the 'factor'. He might function simply as a putter out of work. He might (as in gunmaking) be the organising mind behind a whole complex of manufacturing processes. Among working men some factors had an evil reputation; their nickname — 'slaughtermen' — referred to their misues of their economic power to force down piecework rates. Such entrepreneurial activity hit hardest not the valued and traditional craftsmen but the less highly skilled amongst the work force.

The quality and organisation of life in a Birmingham factory in the 1860s had little in common with Birmingham industry today. In some ways industrial life looked back to peasant independence rather than forward to twentieth-century labour force. Workers in the large factories were often charged for the use of gas or power; operatives were taken on by subcontractors or 'butties', a system still found in the modern building industry. An efficient subcontractor could often make substantial profits — his role was not unlike that of the modern factory foreman except that his allegiance was not to the employer but to himself. Again, industrial discipline was still elementary. Workers would often take off both Monday and Tuesday — referred to locally as Saint Monday and Saint Tuesday, saint's days without a patron saint — and concentrate their working week into the remaining three days. The treadmill of the Victorian factory system was hardly an apt image for industrial Birmingham.

Between the economic structure and the town's social organisation there was a close relationship. Small factories employing less than twenty workmen, a tradition of industrial variety, independent masters and psychologically independent craftsmen, relatively secure in a town with no history of major slump, a town where a break with one employer still left many other workshops open: this was mid-Victorian Birmingham. For the ambitious artisan economic and social advancement lay through opening up a small backyard workshop or by entering the world of the middleman, the subcontractor. Economically and socially Birmingham was a city of small and infinitely ascending élites grouped around local nonconformist chapels. In such a town Thomas Attwood's vision of 'harmonious cooperation' between the classes seemed attainable, and the possibility of a union of 'the industrious classes' more possible than in any other great Victorian city.

Yet the picture of fustian and broadcloth arm in arm in the familial, almost pre-industrial society of Victorian Birmingham blurs many important aspects of the city. Small industry would often mean converted houses and therefore squalid and insanitary working conditions. Paternalism could mean oppression rather than harmony, coercion and not negotiation. Perhaps an indicator of the nature of economic relationships was the lack of a vigorous trade unionism in the Birmingham of the 1860s. Outside the workshop environments were sharply differentiated. At one end of the social scale stood the model suburb of Edgbaston, a well laid out area of houses fit for wealthy manufacturers, and at the other end was St Mary's Ward, with a death rate twice that of Edgbaston. The single-class suburb was rapidly taking shape and Birmingham manufacturers were unlikely to rub shoulders with their workmen in the pub in the evening. Among the manufacturers themselves a ruling élite had emerged: the Kenricks, the Martineaus, the Chamberlains. This élite, and those immediately below, were to be caught up by the missionary zeal of the 'civic gospel', taught so persuasively from so many city pulpits.

The civic gospel gave Birmingham radicalism its cutting edge: the city's political traditions helped to decide its form. From Thomas Attwood and the Reform Bill agitation of the 1830s down to Joseph Chamberlain in the 1870s Birmingham had thrown up political ideas critical of the established order. In the heightened temperature of the clamour of 1832, John Stuart Mill had called attention to the 'most intense consciousness of moral responsibility' of the Birmingham leaders. The great Whig leaders like Grey saw only revolution in the Birmingham plan to set up a civic guard. Yet although the model might seem French it differed fundamentally from the National Guard of 1789. In Birmingham it was to be socially inclusive, not exclusive, a working example of social harmony, of 'union'.

In the 1840s each of the great Victorian industrial cities made its own contribution to national life: Leeds fostered Chartism and Manchester the Anti-Corn Law League. Birmingham under the inspired leadership of Joseph Sturge, Quaker and manufacturer, devised the Complete Suffrage Union, committed 'to unite two dissevered classes' business lions sitting down with working-class lambs. Even after the collapse of the Complete Suffrage movement and of Chartism itself, Birmingham in 1849 was to repeat its call, heard in 1842, for 'a happy union of all classes for the purpose of securing their full and efficient representation of Parliament'.

The tradition reappeared in 1858 with the founding of the Reformers' Union. In the election of 1859 the Union fought for the return of the Liberals, with artisans campaigning side by side with the more prosperous citizens of Birmingham. The most impressive public evidence of this unity was in August 1867 at Brook Fields when 200,000 Birmingham men assembled to proclaim support for reform. Those present covered a wide social range from workmen, trade societies, temperance societies to leading public men. This sense of corporativeness was to have its spiritual correlative in the 'civic gospel'.

The concept of a 'gospel' underlay much of Victorian life. In Manchester the gospel had not been civic and local but national, even international, with a majestic vision of a peaceful, prosperous freetrading England, an England of declining prices, increasing wages and swelling dividends. In Manchester, too, nonconformity had given its moral sanction to the gospel. In Birmingham the vision was narrower, more parochial, more immediate, and was expressed by the great Birmingham divines who dominated the city's intellectual life (7).

Birmingham nonconformity had many mansions. One small but powerful group was the Unitarians. Unitarianism does not stand on the wilder shores of nonconformity, does not produce men of great religious fire. Its passion goes elsewhere, into business, into practical tasks, into educational reform. In Birmingham the Unitarian Church of the Messiah in Broad Street was the intellectual centre of the business aristocracy of the town. The call to action which was the core of the civic gospel could be heard in other places outside Broad Street. One of the most persistent of advocates was the preacher George Dawson, called by Kingsley, 'the greatest talker in England'. Dawson had first preached at Mount Zion Baptist Chapel in 1844 and then in 1847 he had moved to his own Church of the Saviour. From a platform and not from a pulpit, Dawson called on his wealthy congregation 'to clothe the naked, feed the hungry, and to instruct the ignorant'. The civic gospel for George Dawson was expressed almost in Greek terms: for him the city 'is a solemn organism through which shall flow . . . all the highest, loftiest and truest ends of man's moral nature'.

At Carr's Lane Congregational Church another great formative influence was the voice and teaching of Robert William Dale. With Dawson he shared a vision of the social function of the city and saw municipal politics as a high Christian calling. He went far beyond Dawson by calling on Christians to improve the intellectual environment by providing art galleries and public libraries, a policy he described as adding brightness to the life of the desolate.

Within the immediate physical environment of the 1860s nothing called the Greek experiment to mind unless it was the splendid classical Town Hall, the musical centre of the city, built by the Street Commissioners in 1835. Nothing as yet within the framework of political organisation seemed closely related to the Greek *polis*. The Municipal Reform Act of 1835 had set up the ratepayer democracy of the city corporation in opposition to the oligarchic Street Commissioners. This clear victory for radicalism had finally been won when in 1852 the Street Commissioners lost all their functions to the city council. No rapid improvement was forthcoming. The only change was in the size of the town: between 1831 and 1865 Birmingham grew from 147,000 to 300,000. Such an expansion seemed to call for some adequate response from the city council. Instead the hallmark of local politics was parsimony, the frugality which in central government produced a decline in public spending. The 'Economists' in control of the council followed closely behind the Gladstonian policy of parsimony. Faced by the Chadwick revolution of 1848, Birmingham's response was to dig in its collective heels and to refuse to appoint a Medical Officer of Health. Sewage did not excite the City Fathers as it did Chadwick: untreated sewage was still flowing direct into the River Tame and the death rate for the city, particularly in the central wards, was still extremely high.

Although in the 1860s the plea was for sound finance, some change did come. In 1860, the city council decided to build that Birmingham Reference Library which is still one of the great civic libraries, and the civic gospel could further be seen in the new municipal art gallery and in the lending libraries which were to put Birmingham in the van of the public library movement. It was the obstructionist tactics of the key economist, Thomas Avery of the scale-making firm, who both prevented further large scale change, and who by his opposition — as Asa Briggs has shown — made fundamental changes imperative. An enlightened plan to build a sewage farm was held up by Avery who skilfully forced the council to set up an inquiry committee. The report of this committee was as much a revolutionary document for Birmingham as at the national level had been Chadwick's *Report on the Sanitary Condition of the Labouring Classes*. For the committed supporters of the civic gospel it held dangerous evidence of the connection between dirt, squalor and death (7).

If the mood of the 1860s did not fully match the responsibilities of a growing city of 300,000, neither did the meeting place of the Council reflect the aldermanic dignity of the Council. In the pre-Chamberlain era the Council often met in the Woodman Tavern in Easy Row, certainly more comfortable than its little office in Moor Street. Meeting in a pub may be seen as democratic, as relaxed, as inimical to the transaction of effective business. Whatever interpretation is put upon the facts, it is still unlikely that moral earnestness and seriousness would mark the proceedings. For the new men, the revolutionaries of the 1870s, a more fitting background would have to be found: civic salvation could not be found in an alehouse.

2 Liberalism in the 1860s

One of the great and heroic figures of Victorian Liberalism was the M.P. for Birmingham, John Bright. Anti-Corn Law Leaguer, friend and disciple of Cobden, he was pre-eminently a Quaker, with a gift of eloquence which in the decade after he became Birmingham's M.P. in 1858 made him the outstanding radical orator of his age. Honest, just, warm and generous, intellectually he was ill-equipped, after a limited middle-class education, to match the aristocratic leaders of the Liberal Party.

Bright had a dynamism which liberalism had largely lost since the exciting days of the 1830s and a sense of the urgency of the social problem revived in the Liberal Party only with Chamberlain. His stock of political ideas was limited, though surprisingly apposite. The problem in English politics, he argued, was privilege, monopoly; whittle away privilege and English energy would be released over a wider social range. After the Crimean War, and Bright's increasing loss of faith in a middle class who fell in militantly behind Palmerston, Bright took on more and more the role of tribune of the people. Extend the vote in the towns, he argued, and this would make the working class a balancing force to the middle class.

It was in the counties where landed property was still dominant, that Bright thought change most necessary. Change in the countryside, change in the social order, would come from the forces released by the extension of the town franchise.

Bright's liberalism was a creed of attack, particularly in his attitude to the aristocracy, a liberalism of protest, ever conscious of the million poor, yet never able to see the central task: the creation of an educational system which would equip the class he spoke for with the skills and insights necessary if they were ever to take full advantage of a shift in the political balance.

With the exception of Bright and a small group of radical M.P.s, the Liberal Party in the Commons gave no hint of becoming a party of reform. The mood of the 1830s had long since been dissipated and the party was merely the party in power, concerned with finance, with administration, with foreign and occasionally with imperial problems. Its tone was aristocratic - rather more than half of the 456 M.P.s who sat as Liberals between 1859 and 1874 were either landowners or gentlemen of leisure – and its mood was relaxed. Those who were not gentry tried to pass as such and to avoid the vulgarity of radical protest (12, 13).

Although the Whig element in the Commons was small (although strong in the party leadership and dominant in the Lords), Liberal M.P.s were of the establishment, public school and university, and with their roots in land, the Anglican Church, the services. Their concern was to maintain the established order, to avoid passion or partisanship, and to support the administration in carrying forward the nation's business. The commercial and industrial group over the fifteen years from 1859 was made up of seventy-four representatives of big business and then on the periphery, thirty-four militant radical business men, together with twenty radical M.P.s. From this group came the enthusiasms and passion of the Liberal Party, the demand for the abolition of capital punishment, the clamour for a national system of education, and the campaign against church rates. In and out of season these ideas were put forward and met with the bland suavity of the Liberal ruling class. 'The condition of England question' was not at any time in the forefront of the minds of the great majority of the Parliamentary party. Behind the collective mind of the Cabinet stood the country house, the estate, security and a Metternichian certainty of their own fitness to rule. For them the future held no great and noble tasks: the immediate was all.

From such a generalisation certainly Russell, and Palmerston with his support for ending the slave trade, must be excluded. Russell's liberalism often went far beyond that of his party, including Gladstone. On reform he stood for the vote for most of the town workers; on education already in 1867 he was talking of a national system before Gladstone had begun to consider the question. What he lacked was the modern politician's art of courting popularity, to bring together through his own personality the party in the country and in the House; he accepted very few public engagements and his potential as a liberal leader was never fully developed.

Gladstone's position in the 1860s as the emergent leader of the Liberals was still ambiguous. With the repeal of the stamp and paper duties he had stepped into the popular arena, had helped in this way to create a cheap popular provincial Press. From repeal had evolved the liberal *Daily Telegraph* and similar newspapers that overshadowed and diminished *The Times*. In this very important field Gladstone was the man who had taken on privilege and destroyed it. Reports of radical speeches were now widely read throughout the land and political reputations made through the Press. Gladstone in the 1860s was popular in many varied groups and his private benevolences touched many lives. Yet the causes he fostered were economic: the diminution of the state's function his main concern, not its expansion. He had himself adopted the aristocratic tone of the Liberals in the administration and he liked to surround himself with men of good birth. Government, as he saw it, was concerned with the furthering of the public interest: it should rightly be undertaken by those with large responsibilities, large minds and preferably large estates.

As an organised party, the Liberal Party did not exist. The Liberal Party in Parliament differed from the varying and loose associations in the country. There were no headquarters, no nationwide organisation and often little contact between Liberals at Westminster and Liberals in the provinces. Power rested entirely with the Liberals in Parliament. The growing point of provincial liberalism was the Press. Newspapers like the *Rochdale Observer,* the *Oldham Times,* the *Leeds Mercury* stimulated an informed and growing public, readers drawn from the skilled trades (and even in 1866 working men formed 26 per cent of the town electorate), such as joiners, tailors, boot and shoe makers, cabinet makers. Amongst the non-electors militant radicalism remained strong and by issuing lists of black sheep they induced the radical working class to boycott Tory pubs or Tory shops **(12).**

Within a borough, division normally followed religious rather than party lines: the battle was between Church and Dissent. Where Dissent was strong, Liberalism was in control. (There was no genuine parallel in the House where Dissent did not have the numerical strength that it could muster in the country — the religious census of 1851 revealed that nearly half the churchgoing population were Dissenters.) In a largely dissenting borough like Rochdale, the town was controlled by wealthy dissenting businessmen who in effect chose the Liberal candidate and therefore had the power of nominating a Liberal M.P. Before 1867 the normal structure of a Liberal borough would reflect the power of a caucus whose political position rested on Dissent.

Although revolutionary change in the party organisation came only with the National Liberal Federation, organised liberal associations had existed for some time. A Liberal Registration Society was set up in 1860 with headquarters in Victoria Street, London, and was immediately concerned to make certain that potential Liberal voters were on the electoral register. It tried to federate all local Liberal associations and to breathe life into Liberal activity in the provinces. Local branches of the Society became the instruments of provincial Liberal 'nabobs', and even after 1867, when they were reconstructed, the traditional ruling groups often remained in power.

Provincial political activity took other forms. In the north there were many businessmen's and working men's clubs and in some towns in the 1860s Liberal Associations similar to the Birmingham Liberal Association of 1865 sprang up. They seemed not to have been influenced by the Birmingham model. In Manchester, for instance, a United Liberal Party was established in 1862 and similar societies appeared in Wigan in 1860 and in Birkenhead in 1862. Wherever such associations appeared with a conspicuously more democratic organisation, there was — as John Vincent has shown — no real transfer of power from the ruling families.

Through Dissent men indirectly gained political experience. In *Culture and Anarchy* Matthew Arnold pokes a little well-bred fun at a middle class which prefers 'that sort of machinery of business, chapels, tea-meetings to sweetness and light'. But such experience was politically valuable as a small scale exercise in power, in organising, in taking responsibility. In the 1860s, too, the range of this experience was being extended as the religious frontiers of English society were pushed wider during this great period of religious revivalism. This call to religion was not restricted to nonconformity. Evangelical Anglicanism was building churches in the new working-class districts and desperately striving to bring men to Christ. A sense of mission, of life as a struggle for betterment, although shared by Evangelicals, was primarily the quality which distinguished the nonconformist conscience. It was this missionary quality which was gradually to permeate the Liberal Party in the Commons. By the 1860s the process had hardly begun.

The dialogue between Anglicanism and nonconformity often set the tone of political conflict in the nineteenth century and in the provinces the unjust tiltings of the social balance helped to provide support for such groups as the Liberation Society. In the name of religious equality Liberationists were committed to the disestablishment of the Church of England. With a London headquarters, they had a fairly extensive national organisation, which distributed propaganda, intervened in elections, and corresponded with M.P.s to secure a hearing of their case — or a diluted version of it — in the House. In some sense they might be seen as forerunners of the National Liberal Federation in the tactics they used. They represented, in Arnold's term, the Dissidence of Dissent. Their ultimate objectives might seem to be singularly remote from the political realities of the 1860s, nevertheless their campaigns did secure the passing of remedial measures such as the Compulsory Church Rates Abolition Act in 1868, comparable in importance to nonconformists with the financial implications of the

Irish Church Disestablishment Act (1869). By threatening a withdrawal of Dissenting votes, they mustered the support of Liberal candidates a policy worked out in the early 1860s and which brought a harvest of improvements between 1866 and 1868.

Dissent produced the politics of protest, the campaign for social improvement, the demand for the removal of inequalities. Liberalism/Dissent offered the politics of freedom, the freedom of sturdy men who refused to accept the Norman yoke of the privileged classes. Privilege meant established Church and traditional social order of vicar and squire; Dissent meant democratic community of chapel with its political form, the Liberal 'Party' in the country. To be a Liberal meant pledging support in the good fight. Just as African nationalism in our own day gained strength by the very presence of the white man personifying the established order, so Liberalism grew strong in offering an alternative mode of existence outside the social order to its Dissenting supporters. To this spirit, to these groups, and to the provincial Press the new political forms of organised Liberalism could look.

The watershed is clearly the Reform Bill of 1867 which was to reshape mid-Victorian Liberalism (14). From this was to flow all the consequences which floated Chamberlain to the summit of Birmingham politics as the voice of the radical working class. A hundred years after, the breaking up of the log dam seems inevitable. Population had grown enormously since 1832. The towns had swollen and expanded, had often proved incapable of assimilating the new populations, and had failed to provide an environment in which their potentialities could be realised. Industry, steadily expanding since mid-century, had provided work and wages, and slowly improved working conditions. The working man in the towns might be expected to demand some recognition of this economic status, some way in which his social conditions could be improved.

As a generalisation this is open to grave doubt. Certainly in some towns the voice of the non-elector had already been heard as Birmingham's history shows, yet the gulf between provincial society and Parliament was so great that this voice, even if heard in the distance, could safely be ignored. The new clamour, as Asa Briggs has shown, was due to three things. First was constancy of working-class support for the North in the American Civil War. The loss of American cotton had dire effects on Lancashire but not on the steadfastness of working-class support for the North in the American Civil War. This commitment encouraged some English Radicals, and even Gladstone, to point to the outstanding moral qualities of the English working class and to move on from that to ask the pertinent question why they were excluded from the franchise. The second important force was the Italian nationalist and radical Garibaldi whose visit to England was discreetly ended by the authorities, a decision which in turn created a protest committee from which the Reform League was to grow. The third novel factor operating in the mid 'sixties was that first faltering of the British economy which in 1866 produced the collapse of the banking house of Overend, Gurney, and caused rapid and spreading unemployment.

With the death of Palmerston the way was now open for a new Liberal administration headed by Russell to bring in a Reform Bill. There was no hurry. The House returned in July 1865 did not debate Gladstone's Reform Bill until March 1866. Neither was the Bill likely to meet radical demands, disturbing as it was to Lowe and his friends, who thought the way was being opened to the rule of 'impulsive, unreflecting and violent people'. Gladstone's Bill was in fact no more than a minimal concession to democratic sentiment. £7 householders in the towns and £14 tenants in the counties were to be given the vote. Gladstone, the creator of the Post Office Savings Bank, also offered to compensate those who had used this boon and saved £50 by bringing them within the pale of the constitution.

Gladstone's defeat and Disraeli's ever-widening Bill is a familar story: the winter of 1866-67 recalled the worst of the 1840s to the older generation, and the Reform League pressed for a radical solution. To Lord Derby and Disraeli, there was political gold in reform; to Birmingham and Chamberlain, an opportunity for political organisation which was to confirm the worst fears of the opponents of the Bill **(16)**.

3 The Empire in the 1860s

Seaborne empires fashioned by Europeans had existed since the sixteenth century with varying fortunes. Portuguese, Spaniards, Dutch, French, and English had meddled in the politics of India and South East Asia, made treaty arrangements with local rulers, set up 'factories', introduced an alien religion. In the Americas vast areas had been conquered and settled. In the West Indies European colonists had lived on the backs of imported slave labour. Conquest had usually followed trade; protected states were replaced by colonies administered by the imperial power. In the seventeenth century, emigration and the emergence of settler states had set up new patterns of empire and succeeding centuries had seen major wars to decide the ownership of vast tracts of land. Spain's great imperial possessions in the Americas were forced open to foreign trade and finally disintegrated into successor states at the turn of the nineteenth century.

Clearly sea empires depend on fighting ships and efficient merchant marines. The rise of Britain's naval power had ousted both Dutch and French from North America, and during the long wars against the Revolution and Napoleon had added new territories to the empire. The large-scale gains confirmed by the 1815 Treaty of Vienna — Mauritius, Cape Colony and, in 1819, Singapore — provided a springboard for future expansion. By the 1860s England's empire had within it, like appendices, working models of differing types of possessions, each reflecting in their function some aspect of past or present imperial needs. At the base of this extraordinary hierarchy of imperial organisation were the simple dependencies such as Gibraltar and Malta, secured for strategic reasons, with their implied control of the Mediterranean; coaling stations, such as Aden at the entrance of the Red Sea and at the exit to the Indian Ocean; Hong Kong, a trading dependency and also a source of political influence in the Chinese Empire. At a different level of political organisation were the British territories of Penang and the Straits Settlements. Even in the 1860s British traders were looking to intervention in the Malay states, a demand which came to a head in the '70s. In India's neighbour Burma, a slow annexation was already taking place By 1852 the whole of Lower Burma, the area of the Irawaddy estuary, was under British control; by the end of the 1860s British merchants in Rangoon were demanding the annexation of independent Burma in the interests of the overland route to China. If in London the dominating mood was separatist, in the East it was expansionist. Colonies of settlement had also grown rapidly in the nineteenth century. With the end of the first British Empire in 1783, Canada became the chief area of settlement, but the new Pacific colonies of Australia and New Zealand and, after 1815, South Africa, were soon to compete for emigrants. From Britain, convicts, Chartists, Irish, farmers, Highland expellees made their way overseas: frontiers were still open and frontier democracy was a powerful force acting against the traditional social hierarchy which settlers brought with them. Between 1815 and 1890 twelve million British settlers went overseas to help create that Greater Britain so persuasively advocated by Chamberlain's radical colleague, Charles Dilke.

Some parts of the world were not officially under British control but under British 'influence'. In the Ottoman Empire, Britain's 'moment' in the Middle East did not begin until Gladstone's occupation of Egypt in 1882, but since 1841 the Turkish lands had been open to British influence, a region where hopeful liberals looked in vain for the civilising effect of ideas of progress. In China, in some coastal Mediterranean states, in Latin America, British trade, influence and often investment were of political importance.

One great area of the world, Africa, still remained relatively free from influence or control. France had penetrated the Mediterranean coast of North Africa, Britain was powerful in Southern Africa but elsewhere European political power was minimal. Coastal regions in West and East Africa, once important in the heyday of the slave trade, had rapidly declined with the abolition of the trade, although Zanzibar retained some strategic importance as a client state and a part of the Indian defensive system (16).

The London government was traditionally hostile to further annexation: trade and influence were desirable, both carried forward a civilising mission, but annexation meant armies and money (44). To many minds this made sound economic sense for two-thirds of British trade was with countries outside the empire, and half of her overseas investments. Britain's relations with India before the Mutiny clearly represented a differing strand in imperial thinking. The subcontinent was falling more and more under direct control and was of great economic and military value to Britain. Schools like Haileybury were training her rulers and would in turn help to create that high imperial temper of the 1880s and '90s. India provided a market for British goods (19 per cent of British exports) and for the middle class a field of employment in state enterprises, such as railways and education, which in their very existence offer a surprising comment on nineteenth-century Liberalism. India had become the centre of regional commercial expansion in the Pacific, and the Indian taxpayer supported an army used to further British trading interests in China, in Singapore and elsewhere. India's army lay outside the control of the British Parliament and in fact relieved Great Britain of the need to maintain a large armed force to protect trade or imperial frontiers.

By the end of the 1860s the Empire had undergone two major transformations, and the centrifugal tendency which was finally to accomplish its virtual dissolution had already appeared. That Victorian self-confidence expressed most brashly in Macaulay's famous minute on Indian education in 1835 (with its implicit intention to create a replica of Victorian England in the East) had already been shaken by the Indian Mutiny. Institutions were remodelled and the archaic East India Company lost its Indian reserves to a Secretary of State.

The other major change was in Canada. Bryce's *Holy Roman Empire* with its paean of praise for federalism reflected and stimulated the growing conviction that federalism offered the final solution to the problem of politics. Marry provincial autonomy to a central government with limited powers – this was the panacea. American federalism had shown its sinewy strength by successfully weathering a major civil war. In 1867 the federation of Canada was intended not only to reconcile French with British Canada and to weld together a vast underpopulated area, but also to provide a bulwark of British power in North America. With the Durham Report of 1839 Canada had set the pace and pattern of self-government, and she was now given that control of her own policies which Chamberlain in negotiation was to find so inflexible.

Self-government was elsewhere becoming a political reality for other settler colonies. In New Zealand, Australia, Cape Colony - the West Indies had had self-rule since the seventeenth century vested in the sugar planter aristocracy – men of British stock under the lax overlordship of Westminster were running their own affairs. It looked almost as if the Victorian separatists had won the day, men such as Richard Cobden who in 1842 had written:

> The colonial system, with all its dazzling appeals to the passions of the people, can never be got rid of except by the indirect process of Free Trade which will gradually and imperceptibly loosen the bands which unite our colonies to us by a mistaken notion of self-interest.

Why not hasten the day? Why not learn from history, where the evidence pointed to only one conclusion? The revolt of the American colonies,

Latin American independence, the continual assertion of sovereign rights by colonial assemblies, all spelled out the message. The colonial connection cost money, increased the danger of war. In return for this there was only trade which in the normal course of commerce might be available with an independent nation.

Of the many voices raised for separatism, the most able and most eloquent was that of Goldwin Smith, Regius Professor of Modern History at Oxford until 1869. *The Empire*, a collection of his articles published in 1863, set out persuasively his conviction that the military defence of the colonies was costly, that in any event limited military defence was useless. His most telling economic argument was that if colonists on average bought more British goods they did so simply because it was to their own advantage. The objection that, for example, Canadians were loyal and grateful subjects with no desire to be thrown off he brushed aside with the acid comment that 'loyal and grateful subjects of Her Majesty in Canada lay heavy protective duties on the subjects of Her Majesty in England'. There was the further advantage, the unsuspected bonus, that separatism might eventually lead to that 'Moral federation of the whole English-speaking reace throughout the world','a great Anglo Saxon federation may arise'.

Victorian statesmen are not extensively on record on colonial questions although as late as 1866 Disraeli could still be counted as separatist. Writing to Derby he said:

> It can never be our pretence or our policy to defend the Canadian frontier against the U.S. . . . Power and influence we should exercise in Asia; consequently in Eastern Europe, consequently also in Western Europe; but what is the use of these colonial deadweights which *we do not govern*? . . . Leave the Canadians to defend themselves; recall the African squadron; give up the settlements on the West coast of Africa; and we shall make a saving which will at the same time enable us to build ships and have a good budget **(46)**.

Normally colonial debates emptied the House: politicians were indifferent, not active separatists or positive imperialists. At the Colonial Office the permanent officials were often separatists, particularly in the 1860s. Among the politicians there were, of course, men who were neither indifferent nor hostile, men like Russell, Elgin and Carnarvon, radical imperialists such as Gibbon Wakefield, Lord Durham and Charles Buller.

It was, however, at the end of the 1860s that indifferentism was met by active propaganda for a United Empire. In this movement the first impulse came from the Royal Colonial Institute (later the Imperial

Institute) which, when founded in 1868, had the support of Carnarvon, Granville, Cardwell and Salisbury: its motto became 'United Empire' and its meetings the occasion for readings of papers on imperial questions such as 'Proposition for the Reform of our Relations with the Colonies'. The widespread suspicion that the Gladstone government intended to cast off New Zealand strengthened the anti-separatist forces. This suspicion had been nurtured by Britain's withdrawal of troops during troubles with the Maoris and by the cool hostility of the British government to a New Zealand request for a defence loan of £1.5 million In 1869 the New Zealand affair was consistently aired in the Press. *The Times* and the Liberal *Daily News* supported the government. The major barrage of criticism came from the Conservative *Standard* with the Radical *Spectator* joining in. The debate dragged on into 1870 and in the process became transformed into a debate on the value of empire. Newspaper articles and letters, pamphlets and editorials set out both sides of the imperial argument. Already in 1869, one writer, Labillière, conjured up a headier imperial vision. 'I am convinced', he wrote,' that the existence of such a relation will not only be of vast moral and material advantage both to the parent nation and to the offspring nations, but will constitute an Empire more splendid than any the world has yet seen'.

By 1870 the men of Empire had been strengthened by the open support of J.A. Froude, the historian (51), and the Liberal statesman W.E. Forster; by 1871 imperialists were not merely stating the case against separatism, they were preaching imperial federation. The imperialist movement from which Joseph Chamberlain was to draw ideas and support had been born. The Radical Charles Dilke published in 1868 *Greater Britain*, looking to a spendid Anglo-Saxon future and discounting the non-Anglo-Saxon dependencies (47a). This theme of a developing and maturing Anglo-Saxon Empire remained a dominant thread in imperialism. There was, however, the Victorian impulse for humanitarian improvement which ended slaving and slavery, and the evangelical humanitarianism of Exeter Hall seeking to protect the native population against the settler (45). Could these two elements be reconciled? Would the concept of Anglo-Saxondom mean the neglect of the interests of Maoris, of aborigines, of Bantus? (62)

PART TWO

Chamberlain and his times

Chamberlain and his times

4   A Midland Politician

Southgate's book *The Passing of the Whigs* (13) gives 1886 as the formal date for the burial of the Grand Old Party. No man was more responsible for the rapid mortality of the party than Joseph Chamberlain, that remarkable product of the English nonconformist tradition. The nineteenth century had seen the emergence of many such men, amongst them Cobden and Gladstone, but no one who so fully represented the moral seriousness and emotional prickliness of the type, two outstanding characteristics of the nonconformist, characteristics which were to have their effect not only on Chamberlain himself but on the nature and development of English politics at the end of the nineteenth century and the beginning of the twentieth.

English nonconformity, largely Presbyterian, flourished under Elizabeth I despite Whitgift's persecutions, produced its hero-martyr in Peter Wentworth, attempted and failed to push through Parliament large-scale reforms in the Church and then turned to a policy of permeating the Church locally. Its moral certainty, its concern for local organisation attracted the gentry, particularly the risen gentry, as in a later age Methodism was to appeal to another layer of English society. Its watershed was the Act of Uniformity of 1662 which, carried on the floodtide of the Restoration, was to result in the ejection of many able clergy who were unable to accept with good conscience the whole of the Book of Common Prayer. Among them was Richard Serjeant of Kidderminster, who was forced out of his living and went to live on his estate at Hagley. From him descended Elizabeth Scott who married Joseph Strutt, a member of the spinning family. Their daughter, Martha, married Joseph Chamberlain of Islington; the first of three generations of Josephs in the Chamberlain family. Daniel Chamberlain, his grandfather, had been a maltster in Lacock in Wiltshire and his son, William (b. 1713) had moved to London where he had prospered. He had been apprenticed to John Hose, a master shoemaker and a member of the Cordwainers' Company, and a permanent link between that great City Company and the Chamberlains was begun. By William's death in 1788 he had set up house in Wells Row, Islington, and had established a solid business. Joseph, his second son, took over the business from his father and two branches of dissent — for the Chamberlains were Unitarians — united with the marriage of Joseph and Martha. The fibre of the Chamberlains was more resilient than the stock from which Martha came, for the Chamberlains were churchwardens at St Laurence Jewry in the City and it may be that with the union of northern manufacturing nonconformity with City dissent, softened by commerce and the economic need to conform, a tougher strain entered the Chamberlain family.

The second Joseph Chamberlain was born in 1796. From his marriage to Caroline Harben in 1835, Joseph Chamberlain, Birmingham manufacturer and politician, was born. The Harbens had their own distinction. They, too, had risen from a maltster's family, in Southsea, but the true fortunes of the family were founded by Thomas Harben, a clockmaker in Lewes, who in 1747 scooped a fortune from the sea. During the War of Austrian Succession, a Spanish ship had been taken prize and in a gale had been blown ashore on the Sussex coast. Harben bought up the wreck and built Corsica Hall near Seaford out of the silver torn from the sea. His son, another Thomas, became a great speculator, and left thirteen children but little else after investment in landed estates turned out badly. The next generation in the person of Henry, turned once more to solid trade, in beer and then in cheese. It was his daughter who was mother to Joseph Chamberlain the third. It may be argued that willingness to take great risks, as Chamberlain did so often in his career, is something which the Harben inheritance gave him. Stubbornness, toughness, the occasional chameleon-like quality which he showed, the capacity to conform as City dissenters so often had, all these are within the richly varied traditions of English nonconformity—but the willingness to have so much career capital at risk is not.

Joseph Chamberlain was born on 8 July 1836 at No. 3, Camberwell Grove, a pleasant newly built house within easy reach of Cheapside. He was the eldest of what was to be a tightly knit family of nine living comfortably on £800 a year. His last two years at Camberwell—the Chamberlains left when he was ten—were spent at a school run by two sisters, Miss Charlotte and Miss Harriet Pace, and when they settled at No 25 Highbury Place, so relaxed was the family's Unitarianism that he was sent to a school in Canonbury Square belonging to an Anglican clergyman, the Reverend Arthur Johnson. At the age of fourteen he was sent to the most famous of dissenting academies, University College School, then in Gower Street, which, founded in 1830 had under its most capable head, Thomas Hewitt Key, already established a reputation not only for scholarship but, in an age of flogging, for its abandonment of corporal punishment.

At sixteen he left. His mother had wished him to go on 'that godless institution' University College, London, but on simple egalitarian grounds his father refused. He would not for reasons of the mere accident of birth educate his eldest son beyond the level that he would be able to afford for his other sons. There may have been another reason here too. The elder Chamberlain wanted one of his sons to enter the Unitarian ministry and hoped particularly that his firstborn would feel the need to do so, and he offered to Joseph (or any other of his five sons) a settlement of £200 if he would take up training for the ministry. None of the Chamberlain boys accepted the offer. The whole episode offers some comment on the standards of that middle class to which the Chamberlain family belonged. The shoemaking business at 36 Milk Street had been improving steadily and in 1846, six years before Joseph left school, the profits for the year were £1,284. The cost of university education would not have seemed to be beyond the family's means.

Joseph Chamberlain's family shared the liberalism of English dissent. The campaign for the removal of legal disabilities, the belief in the virtues of free trade, the zealous reading of the *Daily News,* all these they had in common with so many other similar families. But they did not accept the Cobden-Bright view of foreign policy. For them the 1854 war against Russia and Palmerston's handling of it was fully justified and here the sharp differentiation between this extreme Dissent and its seeming neighbour, Quakerism, is revealed. As A.J.P. Taylor has shown (94), for many English nonconformists the 1854 war was a crusade against tyranny and those, who like Prince Albert, were apparently hesitant to pursue it were traitors to English liberty. Chartists such as George Julian Harney were to see it in the same way. (93).

Although in later life Chamberlain's capacity for nonconformist campaigning is continually revealed, his uncomfortable zeal for creating popular movements, evident even in his last prolonged illness, his moral concern may not be so clear unless the nature of his family's religious beliefs and practices is understood. The Unitarians' contribution to social reform has been profound and certainly its broad humanitarianism, its concern for good works produced many outstanding Victorian philanthropists such as Southwood Smith or Fielden. The Chamberlains were attenders at Little Carter Lane, Doctors' Commons, near St Paul's, a meeting house which had been founded in 1733, and after Chamberlain left school he taught at a Sunday school in a mission hall supported by the chapel at Carter Lane. Not for the Chamberlains the great social causes but the immediate and practical, teaching, provident societies and later slum clearance and pension schemes. Never the visions of Bright of a world nurtured in free trade and peace, or the wilder shores of English nonconformity: for Chamberlain the work to be done was near at hand.

It might be said that by its very nature, its dilution, that Unitarianism does not produce men of great religious passion: that passion goes elsewhere, into business, into practical reforms, into education as amongst the Boston Unitarians. Yet one of its attractive virtues is that its broadness, its tolerance, allows its members to develop interests which other branches of nonconformity condemn. The Chamberlains shared the nineteenth-century passion for amateur theatricals and for dancing, read the new Dickens as they came out and later in life, as a young man in Birmingham, Joseph took up the fashionable sport of mountaineering.

In the two years he was in the Milk Street business Joseph had a full life teaching, attending science lectures at the Polytechnic, acting and learning the discipline of a job which required attendance for practically every weekday of the year. Indirectly it was the Great Exhibition that changed the developing pattern of his life and took him to Birmingham, where he was to become one of its most famous citizens.

An American invention for making screws mechanically, displayed at the Great Exhibition, caught the eye of John Sutton Nettlefold, related to the Chamberlains by marriage and who, in the 1840s had transferred his screwmaking business from London to Birmingham. The capital needed to buy the United Kingdom rights of the machine was more than Nettlefold himself could raise ˙but he persuaded the elder Chamberlain to come in with him. To represent the family's interests Joseph, at the age of eighteen, was sent to Birmingham to take a share in the management of the screwmaking business (22).

THE MAKING OF A POLITICIAN

In Birmingham, Chamberlain prospered. Gradually the firm of Nettlefold and Chamberlain took over many local workshops making woodscrews. Technology had made Chamberlain rich: he was now to turn to infinitely more complex world of social engineering.

His first major attempt at social repair was in education. In 1867 Birmingham radicals had set up an Education League. Its primary purpose was fact-finding, collecting information which could be set out in their immensely effective pamphlets—for example, that out of

c. 4,250,000 children of school age, 2 million attended no school and another million went to uninspected schools. For Joseph Chamberlain the civic gospel was clear: 'that it is as much the duty of the State to see that they are educated as to see that they are fed'.

The early days of the League recall its great Manchester predecessor, the Anti-Corn Law League. The first meeting of the Provisional Committee raised £7,000, of which £1,000 came from Chamberlain's own pocket. Transformed into the National Education League, branches were established in Manchester, Leeds, Bradford, Bristol, Sheffield, indeed in all the centres of provincial liberalism. At its height the League had one hundred branches when George Dixon, Birmingham's Liberal M.P., handed over the chairmanship to Chamberlain. The League's success in overturning settled Liberal dynasties anticipated Chamberlain's own National Liberal Federation (23).

On fundamentals the League was agreed. Education was to be universal, compulsory and free. Chamberlain was advocating that England should follow the American example in setting up schools on the pattern of the American common school, made widely known in England by the report of the Rev. James Fraser, who had gone to America in 1865 to study American schools.

English nonconformity ranged itself behind the National Education League. To offset its appeal and to speak with the voice of the Anglican establishment the National Education Union was set up and once more the educational debate became part of that dialogue about religion which had marked so much of the nineteenth century.

When Forster introduced his Bill in 1870, education was not to be compulsory or free in either sense for its basis was to be the voluntary school with provision for exemption from religious teaching for dissenting or agnostic parents. Chamberlain headed a delegation to Gladstone to present the viewpoint of the League. Chamberlain was thirty-four, Gladstone sixty and in his prime as politician and Liberal leader: Chamberlain symbolising populace and industry and Gladstone (despite his mercantile background) aristocratic security and the great estates.

The League intensified its propaganda, but in vain. Forster's Bill was passed. The battle then moved to the local level. In Birmingham the new school board set up by Forster's Act had an Anglican and Conservative majority, with a Liberal minority, including Chamberlain himself. The Birmingham Town Council was liberal and nonconformist and from the Council Chamberlain organised a Liberal political machine which in the 1873 school board elections swept away the Church majority [doc. 1].

Clause 25 in the Forster Act was both a stumbling block for nonconformists and a consolation to Church parties throughout the country. This clause empowered school boards to pay the school fees of poor children going to voluntary (i.e. church) schools and unscrupulous boards were prepared to utilise this clause to subsidise church schools. With Clause 25 as a rallying cry, Chamberlain toured the country speaking on behalf of the League. At by-elections, the League ran candidates opposing the official Liberal candidate, a practice reaching a magnificent absurdity at Bath where the League's candidate had his nomination papers signed by Conservatives who carried the seat in the Conservative interest.

To bolster up the Government and Gladstone, the veteran Liberal John Bright joined the administration and in Birmingham's political centre, Bingley Hall, made a rousing speech condemning Clause 25 as an evil principle. Suddenly, in 1874, Gladstone dissolved Parliament. In the general election that followed, of 425 Liberal candidates 200 were pledged to repeal Forster's Act. Elsewhere nonconformist abstentions may have contributed to the overwhelming defeat of the Gladstone government.

During the preceding months Chamberlain had broadened the attack to take in Church disestablishment, the only means eventually by which 'free' schools could be secured. But the defeat of the Liberals in 1874 lead Chamberlain to argue that 'Education for the Ignorant cannot have the same meaning that belonged to 'Bread for the Starving'. This extension of the argument was to affect the rest of Chamberlain's career [doc. 2].

CHAMBERLAIN'S WORK AS MAYOR AND COUNCILLOR

In 1869 Chamberlain was elected as councillor for St Paul's Ward, the beginning of a career in municipal politics which was to transform the city and to make Chamberlain, by nature a halting and fumbling speaker into one of the great debators of the age (10, 7). His reputation initially was made outside the council, in the education debates conducted before and after Forster's Bill and he emerged as the spokesman of dissent and the new urgent and slightly raucous voice of Radicalism.

Of fundamental importance in the process which made Chamberlain mayor was his new political machine, the Birmingham Liberal Association (see p. 34.). Its whole weight was thrown into the school board elections and the municipal elections of 1873: the school board battle was fought with the exultant cry, 'The people above the Priests'. In the municipal elections the shopocracy opposed him with the cry of low rates. Chamberlain's radicals carried both elections and Chamberlain emerged as chairman of the school board with the Bible party in the minority, and as Mayor of Birmingham. For Birmingham the Golden Age had begun and the era of the Woodman (a city pub where council meetings were held) had ended.

Behind Chamberlain's mayoralty was the force of the civic gospel and the nonconformist élite of the town. One other factor was at work: an extraordinarily acute intelligence trained in business. This was to be a businessmen's government but businessmen with a highly developed civic conscience. The theory behind Chamberlain's policy was, as he said, that 'all regulated monopolies should be controlled by representatives of the people and not left in the hands of private speculators'.

The first great campaign was to establish a municipal gas supply. This was no novelty in the England of the 1870s; thirty-three municipalities in England and Wales produced their own gas. It was revolutionary in a Birmingham dominated by the 'economists' who looked aghast at a proposal which would increase the municipal debt from £500,000 to £2.5 million pounds. Chamberlain was confident that selling gas would yield a sound profit to the town. Despite the opposition of the local gas interests the Bill was passed in July 1875 and within the year Chamberlain's estimated profits were shown to be wide of the mark: instead of the expected £14,800 the City made a profit of £34,000. During the first five years of municipal gas the price was twice reduced and Birmingham gas became a model of thrifty and efficient administration.

No such profits could be expected from Chamberlain's second great measure. Sir Edwin Chadwick at the Public Health Board thirty years before had seen the evils of a water supply in private hands. In the Birmingham of the 1870s they were still rampant. The Water Company's piped water supply operated only on three days a week. Half the population of this city of 300,000 had its water from surface wells, some of them discoloured and poisoned by sewage.

Chamberlain's speech in the Council Chamber in 1874 set out its democratic principle of regulated monopolies and pleaded that the 'power of life and death' should not be left in private hands. Why, he wondered sardonically, is not the supply of air regulated by the legislature and handed over to some company with a dividend limited to 10 per cent? His maxim was to be cheap water: he maintained that 'whereas there should be a profit made on the gas undertaking the water should never be a source of profit: all profit should go in reduction of the price of water'. Although this represented a revolutionary doctrine, once again the policy was not a novelty. Most of the large towns of the United Kingdom – Glasgow, Liverpool, Manchester, Plymouth, Dublin - had their municipal water supply. Birmingham's 'gas and water socialism' was influential not because of its freshness but because of its efficiency and the forcefulness of its chief advocate. Water was added to gas as a municipal concern.

His third main achievement lay in building that 'boulevard' (as he called it) that the Improvement Scheme made possible by Cross's Act of 1875 and which created Corporation Street. He introduced the scheme to the Council with a flourish of environmental socialism. He argued that conditions maketh man and 'It is no more the fault of these people that they are vicious and intemperate than it is their fault that they are stunted, deformed, debilitated and diseased'. Again his argument turned on the threat to health, the statistical differences in the death rate in the slum quarters of the town compared with the death rate in Edgbaston. Corporation Street was to be thrust through the centre of the town and some of the worst slums destroyed. Twenty-two yards wide, Corporation Street, treeless, and architecturally diverse was not quite a boulevard, yet it was a clear advance on the rabbit warrens of the streets it replaced.

5 The Radical Revolution

CHAMBERLAIN AS A PARLIAMENTARY CANDIDATE AT SHEFFIELD

Forster's Education Act as a stimulus to radical activity and as a disruptive force in settled Liberalism was strongly evidenced at Sheffield. Here in 1872 the famous Sheffield Radical, Henry Wilson, together with local nonconformist ministers formed 'The Sheffield Nonconformist Committee' with the stated purpose of creating an informal public opinion in the town and demanding changes in Forster's Act.

A conflict arose with the local school board set up by the Act and the Nonconformist Committee asked for the help of their Birmingham counterpart and the National Education League who advised them to refuse to pay the local education rate. This was advice which had been given to other areas in the country and in Sheffield was widely followed by nonconformists with the intention of forcing the Government to give way.

By 1874 and the general election, Gladstone had made no major concessions and Wilson and the Sheffield nonconformists were dissatisfied with official Liberalism whose line was sedulously followed by the Sheffield Liberal Association. Already he and his supporters had made an official break with the local party by forming a splinter group, the Sheffield Reform Association. Wilson found salvation in an article Joseph Chamberlain had written for the *Fortnightly Review*, October 1874, calling in resounding terms for the formation of a new party. The article proclaimed:

> The unexampled commercial prosperity of the last few years has led many to lose sight of the co-existing misery and discontent of a large portion of the population . . . whose homes would disgrace a barbarous country. The party will not be reunited until a programme has been elaborated which shall satisfy the just expectations of the representatives of Labour as well as conciliate the Nonconformists who have been driven into rebellion.

The new party, Chamberlain said, must be based on the Four Freedoms: 'Free Church, Free Schools, Free Land, and Free Labour.'

On the strength of this article, Wilson invited Chamberlain down to Sheffield to meet the Reform Association and Chamberlain, so recently made Birmingham's Mayor, found himself adopted as the Radical candidate in Sheffield. His views were again forcibly expressed in a speech at Birmingham in the same year.

In the election four candidates ran: the sitting Liberal M.P., A.J. Mundella; the Sheffield Liberal Association's candidate, A.J. Allott; the nominee of the Reform Association, Joseph Chamberlain; and J.A. Roebuck, Liberal. Wilson and his friends pressed for the return of Chamberlain and Mundella but Roebuck headed the poll, behind him the Anglican vote and his splendid slogan, 'Stand by your National Religion and your National Beverage', with Mundella as second member Chamberlain was narrowly defeated. He felt utterly humiliated by his failure to carry the seat, as creator of the National Education League, as a politician well on the way to becoming the most famous Radical in England, and furthermore defeated on the Radical ticket of the Four Freedoms. He refused to consider standing again, at least at Sheffield (22).

THE STRUCTURE OF POLITICS

In the ten years after the passing of the Reform Bill of 1867 and before the coming of the National Liberal Federation, little changed in the structure of English politics. These were the years of continued prosperity, years before the agricultural disasters of the late 1870s and the slackening of the English industrial impulse in the 1880s.

In the counties it was still the age of Trollope. English land was concentrated in the hands of the great landowners — 54 per cent of land in England and Wales was owned by landowners with more than 1,000 acres. Small owners were numerous, (as many as a quarter of a million), but apart from such areas as East Anglia where they were often dissenters, they were politically unimportant. The great landowners traditionally had the voting support of their tenants - even in 1868 the M.P. for Huntingdonshire, Edward Fellows, rode to the polls at the head of his 150 tenants, like some nineteenth-century English posse intent on securing justice, in this case the return of their leader. As there were relatively few Whig landlords, the English counties were fairly well held by the Conservatives. Some counties such as Kent or Essex which abounded in small towns were held only by narrow margins, and electoral changes such as the enfranchisement of the agricultural labourer in 1885 could change the whole balance of politics in the county (11, 12).

The urban constituencies varied widely both in their politics and in their structure. At one end of the scale were 113 towns with less than 16,000. returning half of the borough M.P.s, roughly one-fifth of the total membership of the Commons. Towns such as Bridgnorth or Truro or Tiverton belonged essentially to the *ancien regime* of pre-1832 England in that they were subject to 'influence'. The nature of that influence varied from the family boroughs such as Huntingdon, in the gift of the Earl of Sandwich, to Cricklade, virtually owned by the Great Western Railway with its enormous works at Swindon, and with Daniel Gooch of the G.W.R. sitting as its Conservative M.P. from 1865 to 1885. Some small towns such as Bridport were open to the highest bidder and looked to their M.P. to pour funds into the town in return for their electoral support. Bribery took many forms: at Taunton in 1865, of 900 electors 270 made it clear that they would vote only if they were paid; at Bewdley in 1868, Sir Richard Glass spent £4,000 to win the 1,000 electors, and the money provided free drinks in the town's twenty pubs for all comers.

Medium-sized towns with populations between 16,000 and 50,000 numbered seventy-five boroughs such as Ipswich, Cambridge and Lincoln. In most of these towns the largest employer of labour virtually had the town in his gift. The Ferguson family controlled Carlisle; the Brocklehursts, Macclesfield; at Blackburn, two Conservative families, the Hornbys and the Feildens controlled the town. This type of town was usually in the Liberal interest, for many employers and small shop-keepers were Liberal. Workmen voted for their employers, not because of any pressure exerted on them, but because of feudal-type loyalties and inbred respect for the head of the leading local family, and often because politically in such towns employer and operative shared the same political views. Nevertheless it was accepted that the employer had the right to influence the politics of his workpeople and his lesser agents, managers and foremen were normally men of the same political viewpoint who could if necessary carry with them the votes of the workers themselves.

It was in the big towns, in Manchester, Birmingham, Leeds and London, that the pattern of the future was to be seen. Most of the large towns looked to Liberalism, and were hostile to the Conservatives, who were associated in the popular mind with land and the established Church. Up to 1867 the pattern of political arrangements had differed only slightly in the large towns from their smaller counterparts; after 1867 and as a direct result of the Reform Bill, new political forms began to emerge, one of the most powerful an agent of that Birmingham imperialism which came to shake the very foundations of traditional Liberalism. Dissent and Radicalism were to transform English Liberalism.

THE CAUCUS

Birmingham Radicalism was to colonise each of the large towns of England through the thrusting force of the National Liberal Federation, the successor body to the Birmingham Liberal Association. Birmingham had had a long tradition of common action, a tradition going back to Attwood's reform association of 1829 and continually revived. The Liberal Association was set up in 1865 and from it developed the formidable machine which organised the 1868 elections and won Council and school board for Chamberlain in 1873.

Certainly Disraeli's Reform Act of 1867 had stimulated the growth of the Association. Within the Act was Disraeli's late concession giving some large towns three M.P.s. One such town was Birmingham, where voters were given two votes. The Association proved its political skill by organising the wards of the town: in some wards voters would turn out for Dixon and Muntz; in others for Bright and Dixon, and the remainder for Muntz and Bright. These Liberal tactics made Birmingham safe for Liberalism. The Liberals carried Birmingham in all three constituencies by majorities of three to one, with only marginal differences between the first and the third Liberal M.P.s.

However, it is also clear that the Birmingham Liberal Association did not spring to take hold of the opportunities afforded by the 1867 Act. Not only did the Association antedate the Act but also the tradition of political support across the social board was far older than the Association itself. Even the uniqueness of the Birmingham example is more than doubtful. In 1868 Robert Spence Watson organised the voters in Newcastle and Sir Charles Dilke, later to be one of Chamberlain's greatest allies, did the same in Chelsea. F.W. Herrick (14) sees the emergence of such associations as marking the beginning of the alliance between the Liberal Party and organised labour which was to last until the rise of the Labour Party. The real importance of 1867 in Birmingham and elsewhere was the democratisation of the franchise, not the minority clause. The Liberal Association in Birmingham was reorganised to meet the challenge of this fundamental and revolutionary reform.

Organised politics had entered English political life. In Birmingham the organisation was overtly democratic, with elected ward committees electing a central representative committee. This central body was unwieldy in size, 400 in 1868, growing to 2,000. It met eight or nine times a year and its principal function was to choose M.P.s and Liberal representatives on the school board. Set above this body was an executive committee of over 100, which was managed by a committee of eleven, the real heart and mind of the Liberal machine (Ib 17). The emphasis was on democratic participation in political decision-making, and in this sense the Association was in harmony with the new 1867 franchise.

There was a peculiarly Birmingham note struck in the description of the National Liberal Federation: 'The width of the base on which the Association rests prevents the division so often caused by sectional interests' and its representative character is so thoroughly sustained that combined action is rendered not only possible but vigorous, determined and enthusiastic.' This is an extract from the document circulated at the inaugural conference of the N.L.F. held in Birmingham. Altogether ninety-three different associations were represented at the first meeting, from bodies such as the National Education League, the Liberation Society, the National Reform Union and the Land Reform Association, brought in through Chamberlain's friend Jesse Collings who was himself in touch with Joseph Arch, organiser of the Warwickshire Agricultural Workers Union. The original proposal to form so broadly based an association had come from William Harris, a Birmingham architect and municipal reformer, and Chamberlain's decision to take up this idea brought with it two very important changes of direction. It meant first that he had now abandoned specific nonconformist grievances and was moving over to a new radical and aggressive policy. It reflected also the change of direction Chamberlain had taken since he had entered Parliament in 1876. Through his friendship with Dilke Chamberlain had come to understand the importance and potential of organised labour, the force created politically by 1867.

Chamberlain's strategy·in setting up the N.L.F. had varied motives. Gladstone had resigned in 1874, the Liberal leadership had passed to Hartington, a Whig grandee. With a sufficiently bold stroke the Birmingham Radical might seize the leadership and take liberalism towards a new interpretation. Again the Liberals had lost, and badly, in the election of 1874, and the Liberal electoral machine was in need of overhaul. The ineptitude of the Disraeli government in handling the affair of the Bulgarian massacres, and its weakly pro-Turkish policy offered scope for a national campaign. Gladstone, whose pamphlet on the Bulgarian Horrors had so stirred public opinion, promised to attend the inaugural meeting of the National Liberal Federation, held in Birmingham in May 1877. His presence gave the meeting a semi-official sanction. Chamberlain became President, William Harris, chairman, and Francis Schnadhorst its paid secretary. The N.L.F. was never to become as all-inclusive as its founders hoped. Apart from the National Educational League all the other Liberal Associations retained their independence (20).

Gladstone's concern for the Bulgars and the agitation against Turkish misrule had profound implications for Chamberlain. Gladstone felt the cause to be so important that he was impelled to reverse his previous decision and once more took up the burden of political leadership, thus barring Chamberlain's own rapid progress to the leadership of the Liberal Party. Furthermore, Gladstone's involvement with the Eastern Question quickened his interest in the problem of Ireland, the issue on which he and Chamberlain finally parted company (32).

THE NATURE OF THE FEDERATION

This debate over the true nature of the National Liberal Federation often obscured rather than clarified its nature. Gladstone and Granville disagreed about its purpose. Granville said 'that Chamberlain's object is not to reorganise the whole liberal party, but to strengthen the young liberal, and more advanced section of it', Gladstone was sympathetic to the need for 'electoral reorganisation', but hostile to 'the reorganisation of Liberal policy from that centre [Birmingham]' (36, 30).

The Federation was widely seen as the instrument of Birmingham imperialism, as a means of unseating old-style Liberals and replacing them by Radicals made in Birmingham: in fact as a means of carrying out that programme for a new party which Chamberlain had so eloquently advocated in his famous article in the *Fortnightly Review* (1a). Chamberlain's own interpretation of the nature of the Federation was disingenuous. He emphasised that it was a democratic organisation which enabled the whole of the Liberal electorate to discuss policy and to make policy.

Of the many forces which helped to create the Liberal victory of 1880, the strength of the new political machines is likely to have been one. Of the 60 constituencies where there were Liberal organisations affiliated to the N.L.F, the Liberals won 28 from sitting Conservative members, although in Greenwich, Leominster, Maidstone and Sheffield, the Liberals lost 6 seats to the Conservatives despite the active support of an association affiliated to the Federation.

What other forces were at work? Clearly Mr. Gladstone's great moral crusade against Government and Turks, concentrated in the Midlothian campaign, must have brought before many voters the importance of foreign policy, and helped to discredit the Tories. The creeping depression of the late 'seventies did nothing to help the government and the Irish vote in English constituencies might have been crucial in some areas. The extent of the landslide can easily be exaggerated. As Trevor Lloyd points out, it was 'a near run thing' (91). 4,054 votes lost to the Liberals would have lost them 72 marginal seats. In Lloyd's view, 'the depression, the export trade, and the Eastern agitation were linked in people's minds, and it was in the areas where all three factors applied that the Liberals improved most conspicuously on their 1868 showing.'

On the evidence available, organisation alone cannot account for the Liberal victory, despite Schnadhorst's claim which did so much to strengthen Chamberlain's own position.

After 1880 the nature of the Federation changed in that it was primarily concerned to act as a whip for the Liberal Government in office, particularly as its leader was now a member of that Government himself. Members were brought to heel and forced to support the Gladstone government through the operations of the N.L.F. As no election manifesto as yet existed to which M.P.s gave their implicit agreement, the N.L.F. acted as a means of bringing reluctant members to heel.

In Lancashire in particular opposition developed to this new type of parliamentary control, and Manchester, once the leader of radical opinion in the 1840s, resented Birmingham and its control of the Federation. In Manchester the Liberals even went so far as to draw up a scheme of a rival union to outflank Birmingham but it got no support from the Whig leaders who feared that such an organisation might lead to a permanent break in the party.

The debate over the National Liberal Federation had surprising overtones. To the Whigs it was clear that this was the beginning of a takeover bid from the Radical wing of the party. Yet it was more than that: it came to be seen as the onset of Americanisation in English politics. One correspondent in *The Times* begged his readers not to accept along with sewing machines and agricultural implements and tramways, American political machinery as well (31, 35).

This controversy was confused, perhaps deliberately, by the use of the word 'caucus' itself. Within a fortnight of the first meeting of the N.L.F. in Birmingham *The Times* had run a leader in which the new machine at Birmingham had been dubbed a 'caucus' with a reference to American usage. This was clearly misleading for the Federation was nearer a 'Convention', but once the word was used, it stuck and the Press took up the cry of American corruption which the word was taken to mean (30, 35).

The debate was taken up across the Atlantic and in the New York *Nation,* the editor looked dramatically at Midland politics and forecast the emergence of a Boss and the 'spoils system'. To Whigs and Conservatives alike the pattern of the future was clear: politics run by radical machines. Behind this stood the demogogic figure of

Chamberlain, and increasingly a parliament packed with Chamberlain's men, following his whims rather than the general interest of the nation. From such a propagandist interpretation, Gladstone was a notable exception for he did not altogether accept the Whig view of the American system, nor was he hostile to Chamberlain — he had after all spoken at the inaugural meeting.

6   The Emergence of a National Leader

CHAMBERLAIN'S APPOINTMENT AS PRESIDENT OF THE BOARD OF TRADE

In the election of 1880, 'Gladstone and the Caucus have triumphed all along the line', in Chamberlain's words, and despite the Queen's view 'that she would sooner abdicate than send for or have anything to do with that half-mad firebrand who would soon ruin everything and be a Dictator', Hartington's days as leader of the Liberal Party seemed clearly numbered. *The Times* had referred to Chamberlain as 'the Carnot of the moment', and Chamberlain felt strong enough to write to his friend Dilke proposing a pact to ensure the representation in the new Government of the Radical wing of the Party. In short he said he was prepared to 'refuse all offices until and unless both of us are satisfied'.

Dilke was very willing to enter into a secret treaty of this kind. The difference lay in minimal conditions. Dilke was prepared to agree to a situation in which only one of them was in the Cabinet. It does not imply that Dilke thought that the Cabinet member would necessarily be himself and during the crucial period of Cabinet making Dilke went off to France **(19)**.

In the event the treaty was put to the test for Dilke was offered only a junior post, Under Secretary for Foreign Affairs (Gladstone took the view that as a Radical prime minister he should have a largely Whig Cabinet), and his prompt reply was 'What about Chamberlain?' Gladstone demurred. He was after all a very young member of the House who had never held office and it was impossible to put him straight into the Cabinet. Dilke then refused to take office. Gladstone resolved the difficulty by offering the post of President of the Board of Trade to Joseph Chamberlain with a seat in the Cabinet. Four years in the Commons and Chamberlain was in the Cabinet.

CHAMBERLAIN AND 1884

Chamberlain hailed Gladstone's Franchise Bill in 1884 as long overdue justice to the agricultural labourer. At last Bright's vision of the future with the countryside transformed (and therefore transforming the town)

39

(12) was within sight of being realised. The landowners would be over-turned and radicalism seep the hedgerows, and Radical M.P.s would be returned from rural constituencies. Toryism and the power of the Whigs would suffer equally as the new democracy came into its own.

One ironic aside as the Bill went through the House was the Tory attempt to exclude Ireland from its provisions. One Tory, Lord Claud Hamilton, warned that to increase Parnell's support by enfranchising the rural Irish would force Home Rule on the country. Chamberlain vociferously supported the case for Irish equality.

Hartington was hostile to the Bill; the Liberal, Goschen, also opposed it in the Commons. The Conservatives, despite their dislike of the measure, offered no continuous opposition. When the Bill reached the Lords, however, it was held up by the Conservative leader, Lord Salisbury, on the grounds that the Bill gave a party advantage of forty-seven seats to the Liberals and that the Lords opposed it, not through any narrow party loyalty, but because they wished a redistribution Bill to be passed at the same time. Clearly an increase in the electorate from 3 to 5 million required some rationalisation of boroughs untouched since 1832.

The position of the Lords was summed up by the Queen in the comment that they more accurately reflected 'the true feeling of the country'. This was heady doctrine and Chamberlain's response was unrestrained (doc.4). He inveighed against the 'insolent pretension of an hereditary caste' and at Bingley Hall, Birmingham, he recalled the willingness of 100,000 Birmingham men in 1832 to march on London with the clear threat that this might happen again. The tension between the two Houses was as great as it had been in 1831-32.

The worst incident took place in Birmingham, in Aston Park, during a meeting held on 13 October 1884. In the stronghold of radicalism Lord Randolph Churchill and Sir Stafford Northcote addressed a meeting which was broken up by rowdies. The two Conservatives narrowly escaped a rough handling or something worse. Certainly Birmingham radicals had had counterfeit tickets printed and had organised the breakup of the meeting. What is not clear is whether anything was intended beyond breaking up the meeting.

Unknown to Chamberlain the Tory leader Salisbury was already preparing to do a deal of Disraelian proportions. The Committee set up to work out a compromise was chaired by Dilke, and Chamberlain found himself at odds with his friend and political ally, for Chamberlain was all for continuing the battle against the Lords to final victory. Morley's slogan 'mend them or end them' expressed his attitude and caused the Queen to comment with waspish fury; 'The Queen will yield to no one in TRUE LIBERAL FEELING but not too destructive, and she calls upon Mr Gladstone to restrain, as he can some of his wild colleagues and followers.'

Chamberlain's final comment on the compromise that emerged, 'Not bad for a Tory Bill', sums up his final position. The Bill, in his view, was being forced upon the Government by the Conservative Lords, led by a peer (Salisbury) with whom he had already exchanged public threats of headbreaking. It was, however, also the same Salisbury of whom a Liberal had observed: 'I should not be surprised if he were to trump us by proposing to abolish the House of Lords.'

The Bills of 1884-85 revolutionised English politics. The Re-distribution Bill with its concept of single member electoral districts forms the basis of the modern electoral system and the Reform Bill had created something approaching universal male suffrage. Chamberlain expected that the changes in the large towns — London's M.P.s rose in number from twenty-two to fifty-nine and the seven large provincial towns increased their representation from nineteen to forty three members — would swell the radical support in the Commons. They did in fact go Tory in 1885.

THE UNAUTHORISED PROGRAMME

'The unauthorised programme' was given this title by Goschen in a speech at Glasgow on 14 October 1885. His purpose was to underline its difference from the programme presented by Gladstone to the Midlothian electors, which was therefore the 'authorised' programme of the Liberal party. The term was used by J.L. Garvin as if it had a precise meaning and he gave a summary of its contents which is partly misleading in that some of its parts included also the authorised programme and others were elements in Chamberlain's policy which he was gradually playing down or even abandoning (28).

Its origins go back well before 1885, to articles which began to appear in the *Fortnightly Review,* written by Jesse Collings, by Morley, and in particular one article written by Chamberlain himself entitled 'Labourers' and artisans' dwellings'. The article argued strongly for the rights of compulsory purchase vested in local authorities at the market price (without giving any compensation for disturbance) to clear slums and carry through improvement schemes. In 1884 and 1885 he stumped the country developing further these ideas from the *Fortnightly Review* articles which, taken together, represented his programme. In July *The Radical Programme* was published. Fundamentally this was an analysis of some of the ideas he had put forward in major policy speeches in

41

Birmingham (5). One element in a speech given on 5 January 1885 had caused great consternation throughout the property owning classes. He had expounded his theory of 'ransom' which implied that 'society owes a compensation to the poorer classes of this country, that it ought to recognise that claim and pay it' [doc. 5]. It was basically an extension of the 'civic gospel', that welfare in terms of the provision of housing was the duty of the community. To many critics it looked like dangerous socialism, but Chamberlain held that he was 'putting the rights of property on the only firm and defensible basis and preventing that abuse of property' which was the real danger. Despite its florid title the doctrine of ransom hardly seemed revolutionary (27).

In September Chamberlain began a tour of Scotland, setting out what he then referred to as the Radical programme, although the emphases were slightly different from those set out in the booklet which bore that name. Chamberlain's Radicalism in the autumn took notice of the change in the political balance brought about by the Reform Act of 1884 which had enfranchised the agricultural labourer, and his new slogan, 'three acres and a cow', summed up this part of the programme. Chamberlain was now concentrating on three main points: free schools — the abolition of all fees for elementary education; compulsory land purchase so as to provide allotments and small holdings and to recreate thereby on a small scale an English peasantry, and finally a graduated property tax. There was a great deal else: the specific nonconformist grievance of disestablishment, a proposal for triennial parliaments and reform of the House of Lords, but these and other proposals were shelved to make way, as the election campaign developed, for Chamberlain's principal ideas [docs 6, 7].

The situation was remarkable. A member of the Cabinet was publicly fighting an election on a basis distinct from that of leader of the Liberal party and his Prime Minister. Behind him he had the National Liberal Federation and the formidable Schnadhorst: in front of him Gladstone and the moderate Liberals. However, Chamberlain's relations with Gladstone were surprisingly cordial.

On 7 October he was writing to Mundella: 'We shall sweep the country with free education and allotments and the Tories will be smashed and the Whigs extinguished.' On the same day he went to see Gladstone at Hawarden and Chamberlain whittled down his terms for entering a new government until he stood firm only on one principle - compulsory purchase - although even here 'he does not expect wide results from it'. Increasingly as the election approached his references to Gladstone became warmer and warmer and principle was abandoned to tactics, tactics which seem more concerned with Chamberlain's own personal position and future rather than that of the Radicals.

The Liberals won the 1885 election with a majority of 86 over their Tory opponents, the balance in the Commons being held by 86 Parnellites. What effect did Chamberlain have on the counties with his smallholder programme? Certainly apart from areas such as some parts of East Anglia where dissent was traditionally strong, there was no reason to think that the counties would break out of their Conservative cocoon. Yet the counties were where Liberalism did well: the boroughs which were offered no particular prizes by Chamberlain or Gladstone did not line up behind the Liberal Party. The new country voter looked to the Liberals, the borough voter did not.

7 The Challenge

CHAMBERLAIN AND THE IRISH QUESTION

Chamberlain's reputation has suffered more from his behaviour in the Irish crisis of 1886 than from any other single aspect of his career with the possible exception of Anglo-Boer relations in the years immediately before the war of 1899. He has been seen as the destroyer of the Liberal Party, the vindictive attacker of the G.O.M., an opportunist on a par with Disraeli in 1846, as the Birmingham radical, who tried to wrest the leadership from the traditional hands with the support of the juggernaut he had built up from the Midlands. Such a view of Chamberlain fastens on his behaviour in killing the Bill but ignores the extraordinary antics of the Gladstone family, father and son, and the highhanded way in which the Liberal Party was treated by them, and fails to notice the tone and content of the negotiations which Chamberlain carried out with Irish leaders before the actual crisis of 1886. What perhaps is true of him is caught in the comment Hartington made on Chamberlain's Irish speeches in 1885:

> The worst of Chamberlain's speeches seems to me to be the enormous difference between the general declaration of what has to be done and the measures which he proposes (38).

It might be true to say of Chamberlain that he saw Ireland as a rather larger Birmingham with slightly more Irish inhabitants than his native city (2). Local government had given to Birmingham a flourishing civic life and a reform programme which had changed the face of the city: local government could work the same miracle in Ireland. Although he had talked as early as 1879 of 'a modified form of home rule' for Ireland, it was not until 1884 that he began to develop this idea in any detail. In a letter of 17 December of that year, to William Henry Duignan, a radical Walsall solicitor of Irish stock, sometimes known as 'the man on a tricycle' from his mode of touring Ireland, he set out some of his ideas. 'I consider [he wrote] that Ireland has a right to a local government more complete, more popular, more thoroughly representative than anything which has hitherto been suggested.'

What Chamberlain could never accept was the possibility of difference between the Irish and the English which might lead the former to demand an end to the connection. Like the new imperialists what was important to Chamberlain was to maintain the unity of the community of which Ireland formed a part.

> I can never consent to regard Ireland as a separate people with the inherent rights of an absolutely independent community. I should not do this in the case of Scotland, or of Wales, or, to take still more extreme instances, of Sussex, or of London. In every case the rights of country or district must be surbordinated to the rights of the whole community of which it forms only a portion. Ireland by its geographical position, and by its history is a part of the United Kingdom, and it cannot divest itself of the obligation or be denied the advantages which this condition involves (38).

Certainly on the evidence of the last sentence it is difficult to charge Chamberlain with a fundamental change of heart in the debates of 1886. In the same letter he admits, that he has 'no objection to home rule in principle' and then goes on to make clear that what he could not accept was any form of home rule which would lead to separation.

It was no fortuitous chance that 1884 was the date for Chamberlain's more intensive interest in Irish affairs. The democratisation of the franchise brought by the 1884 Bill would have its effects on the Irish position: two considerations were beginning to have some political weight — the knowledge that under the new Bill the general election which must be held soon (and 1886 seemed the most likely time) would increase the Parnellite party in the Commons from sixty to eighty, and the expectation that the strongly organised Irish party in England would hold the balance in several marginal constituencies. Chamberlain's approach to the man on the tricycle might be seen as a Highbury kite to match Herbert Gladstone's own later Hawarden kite.

The Duignan letter set out Chamberlain's own view on the future of Ireland. There was to be an 'Irish board' or 'central board' which was basically to be a legislative body given power over land, education and communications. This new Irish board was to be created by the next Parliament, that is after the next general election, when it was confidently expected Gladstone would finally resign and Chamberlain would be nearer the centre of the party itself (37, 38) [doc. 8].

What the scheme lacked is the support of the Irish leaders. Parnell made it clear that such a scheme was no substitute for true home rule with an Irish Parliament. Parnell's objections to the scheme as a sop were made through the intermediary of the ubiquitous O'Shea, and later Chamberlain was to claim that Parnell's views were not conveyed to him by this intermediary. However, Parnell's objections to the central board scheme had been spelled out in his speeches made in Ireland in January 1885 which were covered and reported in *The Times*. Chamberlain must have seen them and he cannot reasonably claim ignorance of the Irish leader's hostility to what Parnell later called 'a useful and harmless reform'.

Unexpected support for Chamberlain's scheme came from Cardinal Manning, Roman Catholic Archbishop of Westminster who approached Chamberlain's friend, Sir Charles Dilke, and later Chamberlain himself. Manning declared the loyal support of the Irish bishops for Chamberlain's scheme and offered their help in pacifying Ireland if Chamberlain's local government plans went through. Manning also referred to another unspecified source of support which Chamberlain in his *Political Memoir* was to say was Parnell's. Nothing was ever definitely said by Manning and in the light of Parnell's Irish speeches it seems a strange error of judgement on Chamberlain's part to assert that Manning had promised Parnell's acceptance of the scheme.

Chamberlain's central board scheme was finally submitted to the Cabinet on 9 May 1885, when it was supported by all the commoners except Hartington and rejected by all the peers except Granville. The scheme in Gladstone's words was as 'dead as mutton'. This did not, however, prove to be the case, for Chamberlain revived the central board scheme — now renamed 'national councils' - first in the *Fortnightly Review* of July 1885 and then in *The Radical Programme*. [doc. 9]. In neither case was Chamberlain the acknowledged author although it is clear that his mind was behind it.

To follow up this resounding 'blast of trumpets, Chamberlain intended to visit Ireland with Dilke. *United Ireland,* Parnell's newspaper, parried this move by an attack on 27 June 1885 intended to discourage the visit. Chamberlain abandoned not only the visit but also the national councils scheme.

The writing was already on the wall. In Wakefield, a marginal seat with an estimated 150 Irish votes, the Irish National League of Great Britain intervened on 1 July through their spokesman, Thomas Sexton, and called on the local Irish to vote the Conservative ticket. The Conservative candidate was returned with a majority of 257. The alliance of the Irish party with the Conservatives had already begun and no national scheme could touch the heart of the Parnellite demand for Irish home rule.

On 21 November the Irish party called on Irish voters in England 'to vote against the men who coerced Ireland', to vote against the Liberals, that is not necessarily to vote for the Tories although this in fact is what was meant. Parnell's decision was not based upon his estimate of the reliability of Tory promises but upon considerations of parliamentary strategy. If the Liberal party were returned with an overwhelming majority, it seemed unlikely that a home rule bill would be a first priority. If their strength in the House was reduced then the Irish party might hold the balance. The results are famous. Parnell with his eighty-six supporters did indeed find themselves in the key position. The Liberals had 335 seats, the Tories 249. Nothing could be neater, for the Liberals clearly needed the Irish party to form a government with a safe majority.

What must be asked is what part Chamberlain's relations with the Irish party played in this. The national councils scheme had been dropped from the unauthorised programme; Chamberlain had been subjected to a great deal of personal abuse - 'shopkeeping Danton' was a favourite Irish description of a man whose personal relations with Parnell and the Irish party were of the worst. In the elections this counted little, if at all; in the struggles over the Bill rather more. Neither Parnell nor Gladstone made a serious attempt to woo Chamberlain, and this failure to win over the second most important politician in the Liberal party was to prove disastrous (**20, 26, 41**).

THE HAWARDEN KITE

Others besides Chamberlain were interested in a solution to the Irish question. In June 1885 the Liberal government was forced out of office and a Caretaker administration under Salisbury took over. In this government, Lord Carnarvon, renowned for his strong views on imperial federation and for his great success in forging the British North America Act of 1867, was Lord Lieutenant of Ireland. Carnarvon, a pacific, conciliatory man, ill-suited for the hurlyburly of Conservative politics, was concerned to find a solution of the Irish problem in some form of Home Rule. He was delighted to find that Dublin Castle, the seat of the British administration in Ireland, also had many supporters for Home Rule. His concern led to a famous meeting with Parnell, on 1 August 1885, in an empty house in Mayfair, a meeting with no third party present, the purpose of which was to explore with Parnell the extent of various Irish grievances and the policies Parnell advocated for their cure.

This meeting touched on all the problems which lay between the two countries and there seemed to be agreement that separation was not the purpose of the Irish agitation, that what (in Parnell's words) was wanted was an Irish legislative body. What was odd about the meeting was that the Cabinet was not informed that it was taking place nor told afterwards the nature of the discussions. Clearly this was Salisbury's decision. Carnarvon was left with the feeling that nothing really prevented a satisfactory solution to the Irish question and Parnell was was led into thinking that the Conservatives were considering some form of Home Rule **(40)**.

Gossip in Parnell's circle about the Carnarvon meeting soon reached Gladstone and he, too, was to interest himself in opening negotiations with the Irish. From Gladstone's standpoint, it was essential that no word of his manoeuvres should reach either Hartington or Chamberlain who might well find it impossible to accept too radical a change of direction in Ireland. On 7 and 8 October Chamberlain spent some time with Gladstone, but the latter made no mention of the correspondence his son, Herbert, was having with Labouchere, who was the intermediary with the Irish leader. In a letter to Labouchere, Herbert Gladstone outlined policy in three ways: the maintenance of the unity and integrity of the Empire; an Irish chamber for Irish affairs and Irish representatives to sit at Westminster for Imperial affairs. Herbert Gladstone further assured the Irish leader of 'the inherent right of the Irish nation to make a constitutional demand to manage their own affairs in their own way' **(23)**.

On 21 November Parnell ordered the 150,000 Irish voters in England to vote against the Liberals **(40)**. The effect of this decision on the election is difficult to gauge: clearly the Liberals lost some seats. Schnadhorst, the party manager, argued a loss of thirty-one seats although a more cautious estimate is two seats lost. The eighty-six Irish M.P.s held the balance in the House: the future lay with them.

After the election, Gladstone made no move. He waited on the Conservatives to press on with some measure of Home Rule. Within the Conservative Cabinet only Carnarvon wanted a constructive solution to the Irish problem and he was arguing for a joint committee to examine the Irish question.

The political stalemate was to be ended by the Hawarden kite. This statement made to the Press by Herbert Gladstone arose from his conviction that inaction was playing into the hands of Chamberlain and the radicals. Certainly Chamberlain was anxious to keep the Tories in and Gladstone out, and Herbert Gladstone's intervention had the effect of precipitating the inner conflicts within the Liberal Party. It meant now that men had to sort out their allegiances as the possibility of a Liberal-Irish alliance grew firmer. It meant also that the manner in which Gladstone's announcement was made without consultation with his party heightened the suspicion that he was a 'presidential' prime minister and gave firm ground for his opponents to work against him.

GLADSTONE, CHAMBERLAIN AND HOME RULE

After the failure of the national councils scheme, Garvin observed, 'The nationalists he never more trusted or liked.' Chamberlain's attempt to become an Irish champion had clearly failed. Ireland was no longer to be one of Chamberlain's main concerns. When Gladstone at the beginning of 1886 formed his new administration committed to Home Rule, the ruptures in the Liberal Party produced by this change of direction demanded careful handling of the man who was clearly his major rival. In this Gladstone failed and therefore in some sense he was personally responsible for the defeat of the Home Rule bill to which he was committed.

To Gladstone, Chamberlain was no more than a careerist to be treated with chilly disdain by a man of principle. Chamberlain's request for the post of Colonial Secretaryship was disregarded [doc. 11]. To Gladstone's aristocratic mind, posts of this rank had to be reserved for men of the ruling families and he had already privately reserved the post for the ageing Lord Granville. Chamberlain was offered the Presidency of the Local Government Board, redolent of the Poor Law and grimy municipalities. He accepted this niggardly gesture (to Gladstone's contempt) and promised 'to give an unprejudiced examination' to Gladstone's proposals.

After this unpromising beginning, Gladstone bitterly offended Chamberlain in two ways. The first was over Jesse Collings's appointment as Parliamentary Secretary to the Local Government Board. Collings was Chamberlain's henchman and Chamberlain asked for and got this post for him. To his puzzled annoyance, Gladstone agreed on condition that Collings's salary was reduced from £1,500 to £1,200. Behind this was no personal hostility. Nothing but a desire to save the Treasury money and no other incident betrays so clearly Gladstone's obtuseness as a party leader. Again as President of the Local Government Board, Chamberlain had drawn up a comprehensive scheme for local government reform. Gladstone with his mind pinned entirely on Ireland could find no time to discuss it.

On 26 March, when Gladstone revealed the structure of his Home Rule Bill to the Cabinet, Chamberlain resigned [docs. 10, 12]. At no point had Gladstone taken the trouble to court Chamberlain. Indeed he expressed to Lord Rosebery his great satisfaction that Chamberlain had finally gone. With Chamberlain, too, had gone any hope that Gladstone could carry the Liberal Party through Home Rule.

The differences between the two men in terms of the Bill seemed slight. Chamberlain's case rested on the need for Irish members in the Commons and on his frequently expressed view that federation and not the complete autonomy which in his view the Bill granted was the key to the Irish question. During the debate Gladstone gradually changed his ground and was finally prepared to introduce a revised bill. Unfortunately he was goaded by Lord Randolph Churchill into denying that he had any intention of 'reconstructing' the Bill and all his peace moves were swampled by what seemed to be simple obstinacy (42).

Behind Chamberlain's own expressed position was the personal history of the relationship of the two men and Gladstone's total failure to try to win over the Radical leader. What part ambition, injured pride, resentment, a sense of achievement and personal worth overlooked, played in Chamberlain's attitude can only be conjecture. It is difficult to feel that he was standing firm only on a matter of principle.

In the division ninety-three Liberals voted against the Bill which was defeated by 343 to 313. Liberal Unionism was born, a curious amalgam of differing Liberal strands, which increasingly became indistinguishable from Toryism.

In the general election, the Gladstonian Liberals had a 'drubbing' in Gladstone's own words. The Liberal Prime Minister chose to fight the election on the dubious electoral ground of Home Rule for Ireland. The result was perhaps indicative of the gulf between Gladstone's policy and the country: 316 Conservatives and 78 Liberal unionists had a majority of 118 over their opponents, 191 Gladstonian Liberals and 85 Irish Nationalists [doc. 137].

Gladstone did not despair of reuniting the shattered Liberal Party. Chamberlain dreamt of creating a new 'national' party. In 1887 a Round Table Conference met made up of Harcourt, Morley, and Herschell and facing these Gladstonians, Trevelyan and Chamberlain. Gladstone made the fundamental error of underestimating the strength of his opponent's position and the support he could command. Gladstone felt that time was on his side and Chamberlain a lone figure. To Chamberlain his own views were those of the Liberals and the nation. But 1887 failed: Chamberlain was never to create a national party. What he was to do instead was to forge a new and extremely influential role for himself within the Conservative party.

Chamberlain's own great creation, the National Liberal Federation, had in the crisis swung its weight behind Gladstone and expressed its full confidence in him as leader of the Liberal Party. Chamberlain and his friends withdrew from the Federation but surprisingly no Liberal association in the country seceded from the Federation in his support. Shortly afterwards the Federation cut its links with its birthplace,

Birmingham, and shifted its headquarters to London. The reign of Birmingham Radicalism was over. Much of it would be soaked up by the Liberal Party and expressed in the Newcastle Programme of 1893. For Chamberlain himself Radicalism became less and less central to his life and opinions—the needs of empire, the synoptic vision of that Greater Britain, was to take its place (23).

8   The Imperial Dream

CHAMBERLAIN AND EMPIRE

When Joseph Chamberlain became Colonial Secretary in 1895 in Salisbury's government, he was assuming office which he had begged for in vain from Gladstone in 1886. With the appointment to a secretaryship of state he was entering the charmed circle of English government, though in social terms he had long been accepted by the English ruling classes and his habits of life were very different from those of the Radical Unitarian who had entered Parliament as M.P. for Birmingham in 1876.

In offering a post to Chamberlain, Salisbury made it clear that the highest office was open to him, even the Chancellorship of the Exchequer. Indeed Salisbury was concerned that in asking for the Colonial Office Chamberlain was taking a post well below his capacities. For Chamberlain the Colonial Office offered a fulfilment of his imperial vision that no other office could match. 'I said again I should prefer the Colonies—in the hope of furthering closer union between them and the United Kingdom.'

The twenty years since Chamberlain's first entry into the Commons had seen a fundamental change in England's attitude to empire. That imperialsim which in the late 1870s could be seen as an emerging force had now entered into the texture of English life and thought. Goldwin Smith's anxiety to dissolve the imperial bond had given place to Seeley's *Expansion of England* (published in 1881) which expressed a pride in England's imperial possessions and a belief that England was becoming a world state and that her colonies must be seen as extensions of England herself. Imperialism had been born and the word could proudly be used to describe that civilising mission, the establishment of peace and good government which was England's special contribution.

The English public schools were turning out men symbolised by Ronny Moore, the magistrate in E.M. Forster's *Passage to India,* men in whom Victorian self-confidence reached its apogee. For them there could be no question of 'native rights' (although there were odd exceptions to this such as the Irishman Pope-Hennessey, a Victorian Colonial governor), what was important was firm authoritarian government based on English law.

Perhaps this confidence in England's mission owed a good deal to the Victorian sense of progress in which nations occupied different places on an ascending scale. The Victorian purpose must be to raise standards through the agency of enterprise, through investor and merchant, and expanding standards would hasten Liberal reforms. The English concern was with influence and not possession. Even as late as the 1880s James Stephen at the Colonial Office put the official view in that way in discussing the future of Southern Africa: 'If we could acquire the dominion of the whole of that continent it would be but a worthless possession.' **(46)** Yet in the 1880s influence increasingly gave way to possession. Robinson and Gallagher argue that in Africa, at least, the reason must be found in the collapse of coastal regimes such as Egypt and Britain's consequent need to think in strategic terms about the Mediterranean and the Far East **(45, 46)**.

Certainly the process of devolution had come to an end. In Southern Africa, Rhodes had begun after 1888 to lay the foundations of what today is Rhodesia; Fort Salisbury was created in 1890; in West Africa after the Berlin Agreement of 1884 the British Government set up its protectorate over the Niger Coast; in East Africa by the end of the 1880s British influence was being exerted in Uganda. A similar pattern was beginning to appear elsewhere. India's neighbours were being annexed to the Empire (Burma in 1886) and in the Far East areas such as Sarawak were brought under British protection.

Annexation of new territories was often pressed on the British government by a combination of local interests, usually merchants who wanted the stability and protection that British rule guaranteed. Such acquisitions brought with them imperial responsibilities, for once an area was taken over it was impossible to think it would be handed back. Imperial responsibilities carried with them responsibilities to the local population which, as mid-Victorian thinkers had warned, could be costly, for they would gradually involve a recognition to provide defence and social services.

The kingdom that Chamberlain surveyed contained eleven self-governing colonies covering 7 million square miles and with a white population of 11 million. The colonial dependencies extended to roughly half that size. Chamberlain might argue that England benefited from her colonial Empire, yet the figures for trade told against this comforting belief. In 1900 British trade with the foreigner was £711 million; with her colonies it was only £237 million. Chamberlain was to bring to the Colonial Office a sense of Empire as investment, or donning the role of Radical mayor, slum clearance areas which could be successfully modernised and made to yield a profit.

There was, however, another doctrine which he developed in a speech in 1893, the doctrine of the estate held for posterity.

> Does my honourable friend believe, if it were not for the gigantic· foreign trade that has been created by this policy of expansion, that we could subsist in this country in any kind of way? . . . Does he think that we could support in these small islands forty millions odd people without the trade which has been brought to us by the action of our ancestors, who in centuries past did not shrink from making sacrifices of blood and treasure and who were not ashamed to peg out claims for posterity? . . . when our ancestors pegged out claims for us in many parts of the world, these were not at the time more promising than the claims which we were marking out.

The language was of the mining camp, of the Klondyke but the call to responsibility was unmistakable.

In a circular sent to colonial governors, Chamberlain was to open up a theme which increasingly came to occupy his mind. He wrote:

> I am impressed with the extreme importance of securing as large a share as possible of the mutual trade of the United Kingdom and the Colonies for British producers and manufacturers. . . . I wish to investigate thoroughly the extent to which, in each of the Colonies, foreign imports of any kind have displaced or are displacing similar British goods and the cause of such displacement.

Garvin comments on the practicality of Chamberlain's approach for his letter is accompanied by a questionnaire framed to find out where British goods are being edged out of colonial markets and asking for specimens of more successful foreign products (56).

The paradox of Britain's Empire had always rested on the contrast between her policy in India and elsewhere; in India, state enterprise, elsewhere private enterprise. Chamberlain, it might be argued, was to bring closer the two concepts of empire. With the experience of municipal enterprise in Birmingham to guide him, he argued that much improvement in the Empire was outside the scope of private enterprise. The vision which lay behind his great Birmingham reforms had power to inspire him still. In the colonies social justice must be established, his special aim must be to deal with the traffic in liquor and to abolish slavery and forced labour.

THE IMPERIAL TEMPER

Before his appointment Chamberlain had already committed himself to the intoxicating idea of welding together 'the great independencies of the British Empire into one supreme and Imperial Parliament' – with the further promise that 'all should be equally responsible, that all should have a share in the welfare, and sympathise with the welfare of every part'.

Both Salisbury and Balfour, J.E. Kendle points out, (57) assumed that the Colonial Secretary wished to restore the old system of British ascendancy and colonial subordination', although in fact this was far from Chamberlain's mind. His policy was always tractable and conciliatory rather than autocratic and imperious.

There had indeed been a significant change in the attitude to empire in the years since the foundation of the Imperial Federation League. Advocated by men such as Rosebery and Asquith, Liberal Imperialism had emerged as an increasing concern for social reform at home, linked with a conviction that 'the condition of England' question could partly be solved by paying more attention to those 'undeveloped estates' overseas. Another strain in this attitude was that Chamberlain-Dilke certainty 'of the greatness and importance of the destiny which is reserved for the Anglo-Saxon race which is infallibly destined to be the predominant force in the future history and civilisation of the world' (46).

The imperial temper of the 1890s had many other elements within it: the socialist concern for the maintenance of humanitarian standards which could be achieved by extending the imperial connections; the Liberal-Fabian anxiety to protect the interests of the native populations against the encroaching settlers; the antislavery lobby conviction that the British flag wherever it flew would stamp out slavery. One other concern which was to become more and more important was the demand for the improvement of trade. Separatism had been fed by the easy assumption that Britain's trading supremacy was perpetual, that free trade would be the main commercial characteristic of a British dominated world, and that in such a world colonies brought no real advantages. This certainty had been shaken by the trade depression of 1868 which generated the first active anti-free-trade movement. Based initially on Manchester, the 'Revivers of Trade Association' argued for reciprocity in duties, that free trade should be imposed on other countries by punitive and retaliatory taxation. The idea spread to Chambers of Commerce throughout the country and then died away with the improvement of trade in the 1870s. (47a)

In 1881 the movement reappeared with new and remarkable

vigour. Again depression had stimulated its growth. Industry and trade had become depressed in 1876, a phase which lasted until 1879; furthermore in 1878 agriculture was first hit by the import of wheat from the transatlantic prairies. This sapping of Victorian self-confidence led to the formation in London on 31 May 1881 of the National Fair Trade League. Amongst its several objectives there were two which echoed the new ideas of empire:

(1) to develop the resources of our own Empire and to determine the flow of British capital, skill, and industry henceforth into our own dominions instead of into foreign protective states, where it becomes a force commercially hostile to us; and (2) thus to transfer the great food-growing industries which we employ, from protective foreign nations who refuse to give us their custom in return, to our own colonies and dependencies, where our goods will be taken, if not 'duty free', yet subject only to revenue duties almost unavoidable in newly-settled countries, and probably not equal to one third of the protective duties levied by the United States, Spain, Russia, etc.' **(49)**.

This fair-trade programme was to figure prominently in the discussions of the Royal Commission on the depression of trade set up in 1886. A minority report actually recommended a fair trade solution with a 10-15 per cent tax on all articles manufactured in foreign countries. In the evidence submitted to the commission from Chambers of Commerce, Birmingham, among other iron and steel regions, called for closer commercial connections with the colonies as a major solution to the problem of trade depression and unemployment. What had begun as a movement for imperial integration conceived as a political advance was now beginning to move out from imperial theorists to the business men and the depressed areas, **(48, 49)**.

One further major strand in the growth of imperialism was the concern for imperial defence. The *Kriegsverein* as Salisbury called it came to be seen as increasingly made necessary by the rapid expansion of the Empire itself and the similar expansion of the German and French empires. Imperial responsibilities argued for a share in the cost of armaments; was there any obvious reason why Britain should bear the total cost of an imperial navy which might be used to shield Australia against German expansionism in the Pacific? It was precisely this problem which troubled the first Colonial Conference in 1887 and produced nothing as grand as a union for defence but a recognition of the principle that Australia should bear a small percentage of the cost of a new Australian

Squadron and that this squadron should not be used outside Australian waters without the consent of the Australian colonies. It was Hofmeyr from Cape Colony who proposed an imperial tariff to be used not only to promote closer union but also to pay for imperial defence.

COLONIAL CONFERENCE OF 1887.

This conference owed its inception to the work of the Imperial Federation League. Founded in 1884, the League, despite its name was not completely committed to federation, and in fact many different schemes were canvassed. Rosebery was its chairman in 1886 when the League assembled in London its first imperial exhibition, the Indian and Colonial Exhibition, which by the time its doors were closed had been visited by five and a half million people. Its popularity was not the most remarkable fact about this intensely propagandist display: what was far more important was the holding of a conference of British and overseas members of the League. This conference called for a League deputation to ask the Prime Minister for two important needs: to place 'upon a satisfactory basis the defence of the ports and commerce of the Empire in time of war' and to find means of 'securing the closer federation or union of all parts of the Empire'. From this deputation arose the Colonial Conference of 1887, invitations for which were sent out three months after the deputation had visited Downing Street.

COLONIAL CONFERENCE OF 1897

Unlike Salisbury, Chamberlain favoured an Imperial *Zollverein*, not *Kriegsverein*. He thought that a commercial union would give an opportunity to call together representatives from the 'States of the Empire' which could lead on to an Imperial Council. In a speech in June 1896 he expressed his hope that such a Council would finally become an imperial federal parliament (57).

An opportunity to test his views against the realities of 'colonial nationalism' came in 1897. It was the year of the old Queen's Diamond Jubilee and the Empire had gathered in London to pay homage to her. The Colonial Secretary decided against calling a formal colonial conference. Instead he proposed an 'informal discussion' with the colonial premiers. The invitations were received with mixed feelings in the Colonies, ranging from downright opposition in New Zealand (although the New Zealand Premier, Richard Seddon was himself a supporter of an imperial council), to Tasmania where Sir Edward Braddon was convinced of the need for an Imperial Parliament. Laurier in Canada indicated that Canada was content with the existing arrangements.

When the meeting opened Chamberlain in his first speech proposed 'a great council of Empire'. The support for this idea was scanty, and support for the far stronger idea of a Federal Parliament was even less. The best that could be done, on Chamberlain's suggestion, was to pass a resolution to satisfy 'the Empire League, and this, that and the other League' that the existing political relations were 'generally satisfactory under the existing condition of things'. Beyond this all that Chamberlain achieved was a resolution calling for 'periodical conferences of representatives of the Colonies and Great Britain for the discussion of matters of common interest'. The colonial conference thenceforwards was to become the means by which colonial opinion was to be tested and some kind of imperial forum created.

Certainly Chamberlain and the Imperial Federation League had misread the nature of colonial sentiments. True, there were certain local difficulties. No overhaul of imperial machinery was practical until the Australian and South African colonies had federated. But more important than this, the Canadian Premier Laurier, who had been looked on before the conference as a potential ally, spoke ambiguously. In practical terms Laurier was content with the resolution applauding the existing relations and all the Australian premiers (except Braddon of Tasmania) were uniformly hostile to a closer connection.

Neither in the field of imperial defence nor in the field of commercial relations was there any movement forward: only the British government, together with New Zealand's Prime Minister, Seddon, and Tasmania's Braddon, seemed to want to change **(57)**.

CHAMBERLAIN'S IMPERIAL REFORMS

As Colonial Secretary, Joseph Chamberlain made important advances within the Empire less immediately controversial than his South African policy but perhaps of more lasting significance. One such was his work to improve public health in the colonies. Chamberlain induced the Royal Society to set up an investigating committee into tsetse fly infestation when he received the urgent report from Surgeon-Major David Bruce on the problem in Zululand. After five years' work this Committee discovered that the scourge of sleeping sickness came from the same species which had played such havoc amongst cattle and horses. One of the great plagues of Africa could now be confronted.

Again it was on Chamberlain's initiative that Patrick Manson was appointed Medical Adviser to the Colonial Office. Manson had worked

58

for years in China and was a pioneer in tropical medicine who had discovered the relationship between the spread of elephantiasis and the mosquito. One of his students, Ronald Ross, working in India had in 1897 discovered that malaria was mosquito borne. In a public speech at St George's Hospital, Manson had called for a new attitude towards tropical medicine. Chamberlain took up this cause, secured some Treasury support and tapped private benefactors such as the ship-owners. The result was the London School of Tropical Medicine, which opened in 1899 **(56)**.

1 At the same time as his initiative in London, Chamberlain had sent out a circular to the General Medical Council and to the medical schools throughout the country. In Liverpool the response was immediate, largely due to the initiative of Sir Alfred Jones of the Elder Dempster Line. There through private resources alone, for no central government funds were forthcoming, the Liverpool School of Tropical Medicine was founded, with Ronald Ross as its guiding spirit. Indeed the Liverpool School opened its doors before its rival in London.

One other major contribution Chamberlain made in this field was his encouragement to the Royal Society to set up a Malaria Committee, partly financed from public funds, to supervise research in India and Africa. Chamberlain's interest led to the first anti-malaria campaign when Ross led teams out to Sierra Leone, to drain the breeding places of the malaria-carrying mosquito **(59)**.

The implications of Chamberlain's undeveloped estates theory can best be seen in practice in the West Indies. West Indian sugar had fallen on hard days. Hit first by free trade, the West Indies had been further disastrously affected by the growth of the beet sugar industry in Europe, heavily subsidised by European governments. West Indian cane sugar was forced out of British markets. To meet the desperate West Indian situation, with islands given over to abandoned plantations and unem-ployment, Chamberlain in 1897 appointed a Royal Commission. Its report looked to the establishment of an improved economy, particularly proposing the creation of a peasant proprietary, better communications between the islands and the encouragement of an alternative fruit trade.

Seizing on these findings, Chamberlain tried out peasant holdings in St Vincent and Dominica and recommended adoption of the plan elsewhere. To make it effective he set up the Agricultural Department of the West Indies and made Dr Morris of Kew its director. From its headquarters at Barbados, the Department's officials travelled through-out the islands giving advice, delivering lectures and teaching teachers how to give lessons in agriculture.

By giving financial help towards establishing fortnightly steamer services between the islands, Chamberlain helped to improve communications. One important link was to improve West Indian shipping to Britain and America. Again Jones of Elder, Dempster came to the rescue. With a small government subsidy he created a fortnightly service, soon increased to a weekly service, between Jamaica and Britain. Jones had a vision of a great development in the trade in fruit and in tourism. Similar improvements were made between the West Indies and Canada, again with a subsidy. America then followed by developing her own shipping lines to have some share in the fruit trade, which by 1914 had become the world's largest.

SOUTHERN AFRICA

In the way of federation of Southern Africa under the British flag stood the South African Republic and the Orange Free State, both entirely surrounded by British held territory, with no access to a port except through Portugal's colonies in Southern Africa. Once already, in 1877, the Transvaal had been under British control when the state was formally annexed to Great Britain. Then after the British defeat of the Zulus, the Boers in the Transvaal rose against the British and secured independence at the Treaty of London in 1881.

In the last twenty years of the nineteenth century the character of the Transvaal had changed a great deal. Powerful mining firms, Rhodes Consolidated Gold Fields and the even greater Wernher Beit and Co., had moved in, bringing with them foreign labour and skilled men. Johannesburg had become a boom town. Founded in 1886, within ten years it had a white population of over 50,000 of whom only 6,205 were Transvaalers (63). Concessions to provide water, to build railways to provide dynamite had been farmed out to various foreign interests, while great capitalists, German and British, had gained positions of major importance in the state.

It used to be assumed that this change in the structure of the Transvaal had resulted in the overwhelming, numerically, of the Boer population by the Uitlanders. A figure of ten foreigners to one Boer was not uncommonly cited. However, Professor Marais argues (63) that in 1899 there were probably more Boers than Uitlanders, an argument which weakens the Uitlanders' claim on the one hand and makes President Kruger's fear of a loss of the Boer character of the state less well founded [doc. 14].

The key to Chamberlain's own policy in Southern Africa lay in the British South Africa Company and the dominant personality of Cecil

Rhodes, British imperialist and capitalist.

Diamonds and gold changed the nature of the Boer state of the Transvaal, and Kimberley for diamonds and Johannesburg for gold far outshone Pretoria as Transvaal towns. Great fortunes were made by men like Barney Barnato and Cecil Rhodes, and the agricultural state of the Boers was rapidly being overshadowed by the new commercial world of the mining companies. British policy looked towards the possibility of union in Southern Africa and in 1874, Carnarvon who had successfully brought about Canadian federation, tried to persuade South African states to meet to talk of possible union.

After the gold rush of 1884 the Transvaal government's revenue boomed and gave the farmer state a financial independence based on taxation on the mining companies. This independence was put at risk by Cecil Rhodes, after 1887 Cape Colony's prime minister. Rhodes had made an enormous fortune out of gold and diamonds and was pursued by a vision of British power securely established in Southern Africa.

With the assistance of the British government, he secured almost complete encirclement of the Transvaal and then tried to induce the Boers to join a union. Having failed in this he helped to float a conspiracy to overturn the Boer government and to put in power an administration more sympathetic to Britain—and to the mining companies. This plan had two aspects: a rising in Johannesburg to be organised by the Johannesburg Reform Committee, coupled with an invasion of 500 volunteers led by his agent Dr Jameson. How far was Chamberlain aware of the intention of the mining companies such as the Gold Fields Company, Wernher Beit and others to organise a conspiracy in Johannesburg?

Garvin writes that 'Chamberlain was undoubtedly providing and was bound to provide for the contingency of a Johannesburg revolution. All information led the Colonial Office to expect a genuine rising for reform— a democratic movement of the old kind with which Liberals were wont to sympathise' (22). Van der Poel sees Chamberlain as 'hurrying up the Revolution' (65). Certainly the conspirators' plans were affected by the Venezuelan crisis and what seemed to be the possibility of war. Chamberlain in a telling phrase (in a letter dated 18 December 1895) said: 'It seems to me that either it should come *at once* or be postponed for a year or two at least.' This evidence Marais examines and accuses Chamberlain of 'actually collaborating with him [Rhodes] to the extent of giving him advice as to the date of the rising'.

On 26 December Chamberlain informed Salisbury that there would probably be a rising in Johannesburg in the next day or two. 'If the rising is successful it ought to turn to our advantage.'

Chamberlain was prepared to throw a blanket of respectability over the conspiracy, to recognise the new government, to move towards a federated South Africa, [docs 15 & 16]. The Raid was a fiasco, the conspirators fainthearted, and the subsequent inquiry in exonerating Chamberlain of blame, blackened Britain's reputation in the eyes of the Boers. The Raid led to frantic arms buying by the Transvaal government to prepare themselves for what came to be regarded as an inevitable trial of strength.

Joseph Chamberlain's great dream of empire bonded together by institutions, by trade, by expanding communications, by Britain's zeal for improvement translated to foreign soil had faltered, faced by the practical difficulties of the colonial conferences. The Jameson Raid and its almost inevitable consequence, the South African War, aimed at setting up a southern Africa united in the British interest. However, the war put paid to the whole euphoric mood of imperialism; the revelations of the realities behind the dream, the concentration camps, damped public ardour for imperial expansion. It was the end of an era, even though the immediate unity of South Africa was achieved.

What responsibility did Chamberlain bear for the Raid (64,65,66, 67,72)? He described it as 'a disgraceful exhibition of filibustering'. In fact he not only denied all responsibility but also all foreknowledge. To the House of Commons (13 February 1896) he said: 'I say to the best of my knowledge and belief that everybody, that Mr Rhodes, that the Chartered Company, that the Reform Committee of Johannesburg, and the High Commissioners, were all equally ignorant of the intention and action of Dr. Jameson's'.

The House of Commons Inquiry exonerated Chamberlain and Garvin accepted this view. 'He had [says Garvin] not a shadow of complicity with the Raid.' Garvin's confidence has not been altogether maintained by two recent South African historians, Jean van der Poel and Professor Marais (73,65,63).

In Garvin's assessment two main factors are overlooked: the course of events leading up the Raid and the relationship between the Raid and the Rising. The Jameson Raid was made possible by the transfer of Pitsani, a strip of territory in Bechuanaland, to the British South African Company, Rhodes's own organisation. It was in Pitsani that the Company stationed an armed band ready for the invasion of the Transvaal. The Colonial Office had been responsible for the transfer. Van der Poel describes Chamberlain's attitude as one of 'official ignorance and private sympathy'. Marais goes much further. In his indictment he asserts that, 'being acquainted with Rhodes's object, he did, in fact facilitate the transfer of the territory Rhodes needed and that he deliberately left Rhodes a free hand to use his troops'.

CHAMBERLAIN AND THE WAR

Four years after what the *Cambridge History of the British Empire* (45) calls 'the unbelievable folly of the Raid', Britain was at war with the Transvaal and the Orange Free State. As Robinson and Gallagher point out the general view was that the Transvaal was 'the richest spot on earth' and therefore should be incorporated (46).

Incorporation into a federal South Africa is the key to Chamberlain's policy. There was no public demand for war in Britain; commercial reasons did not weigh heavily, as British exporters already enjoyed a monopoly of trade with the Transvaal and certainly intervention was not needed to make the Transvaal a ripe field for British investment. Before the war Chamberlain had pressed for an ultimatum to be sent on three separate occasions because he was fearful of a growing republicanism stimulated by commercial success. The Cabinet as a whole had come to mistrust the Johannesburg factions. What weighed with Salisbury, Hicks Beach, Goschen and Balfour were the potentialities of the Cape Town naval base if in a European war the safety of the Suez route was jeopardised (68, 56).

The war was fought to establish imperial control in Southern Africa. In the words of Robinson and Gallagher: 'The empire went to war in 1899 for a concept that was finished, for a cause that was lost, for a grand illusion.' Certainly it is unthinkable that a similar war would have been fought to restore imperial control in Canada or Australia.

Ironically, this war to further Chamberlain's concept of empire helped in the incident of the concentration camps to discredit the whole concept of empire and to contribute in England to a growing cynicism towards empire and a desire to test practice against imperial dream (47 & 50).

9   Corn, Trade and Faction

THE CORN DUTY

It was at the Colonial Conference of 1902 [docs 18, 19] that, writes Amery, Chamberlain was 'in the process of reaching a decision on the matter of reciprocal preference'. Laurier, the Canadian Premier, had been told on the eve of the Conference of a proposal put forward by the Colonial Secretary in which Canada would put some British goods on the free list, and in return Britain would exempt Canadian corn from the Corn Duty (22), vol. 50.

The corn duty had been imposed by Hicks Beach in 1902 to meet the rising costs of the war. To remit the corn duty in favour of Canada would be a step towards imperial preference and on 21 October 1902 Chamberlain put his proposal to the Cabinet. No decision was taken then but a further Cabinet discussed the issue again in November and by a majority the Cabinet decided to remit the corn tax in favour of Canada. The major opposition to Chamberlain's proposal came from Ritchie, Chancellor of the Exchequer. During Chamberlain's absence in South Africa Ritchie was able to raise the matter yet again and on the grounds of the seriousness of the implications of the Cabinet's decision he urged that the former decision be abandoned. Balfour, now Prime Minister, gave way when faced by Ritchie's threat of resignation. He communicated to Chamberlain, then at Madeira on his way home, the nature of Ritchie's opposition. In Balfour's view, the dislocation caused by losing his Chancellor, two months before the Budget (it was then February), was too great to be borne.

There is no evidence that the majority for preference in November had changed its mind: the ball clearly lay in Balfour's court. Not until the Cabinet meeting of 17 March was the matter of the corn duties finally raised when the Chancellor produced his Budget proposals. To the surprise of the entire Cabinet, Ritchie proposed to abandon the corn duty entirely. Chamberlain, perhaps unwisely, decided to give way to the Chancellor—Balfour, despite the majority view was unwilling to throw his weight behind Chamberlain. As a matter of political tactics, Chamberlain should perhaps have forced Balfour to choose between himself and Ritchie by threatening to resign. He chose to fight another day. (95)

With his speech at Birmingham on 15 May 1903 [**doc 21**] Chamberlain entered the lists once more. He came out for imperial preference in one of the greatest speeches of his career. To woo the working-class voter he threw out a promise that preference would be linked with major social reforms, for such reforms would be simple equity as the cost of preference would fall on the working class. In the Commons Chamberlain proposed that old age pensions should be linked with fiscal reform and urged that the colonies asking for preference should get a clear reply from the electorate.

Chamberlain's political tactics were clear: he was appealing over the heads of the government to the electorate to secure support for preference. Balfour desperately tried to hold the balance between Chamberlain and the free traders within the government and within the Unionist Party by his proposal that no actions should be taken until after a general election, when there would be time for an inquiry.

In the meantime Chamberlain and his supporters were mounting a propaganda campaign in the country. The distinction in his mind between preference and protection was growing thin. By August he was prepared to argue for some measure of protection in the interests of of home manufacture to offset German competition [**doc 17**] (77).

In his Birmingham speech, Chamberlain had declared that 'a review of our fiscal system was necessary and desirable'. As a major government spokesman, he could well be seen as presenting a new phase of government thinking on the fiscal question, yet behind him was a divided Cabinet, a divided Unionist party and certainly an unconvinced country.

On 28 May Balfour rose in the House to explain the view of his government. He first of all advocated the use of retaliatory tariffs. He then went on to ask whether there might not be fiscal arrangements devised 'to bind the colonies and the Empire closer together', and he recommended preliminary collection of evidence. Then if public opinion moved in this direction 'we ought to do something to put the British Empire in an economic position which would make it an equal to the magnificent position obtained by the United States'.

Although Chamberlain saw revision of the fiscal system as a means to unite the Empire, he was also concerned to parry the argument that this would mean dearer food (by a preferential tax on corn), by coupling preference to major expenditure on social services. However by July 1903 he was arguing the case for economic expansion, which might be one of the consequences of a new fiscal system. From the sugar industry he cited evidence to show that free trade had restricted the growth of sugar refining in England. 'Other countries have been increasing rapidly while we have remained stationary.' In this argument appears the more openly protectionist line marking his speeches after his resignation.

Chamberlain's clarion call had brought over to his side almost all the Unionist Press. *The Times*, the *Daily Telegraph*, the *Daily Express* and finally, the *Daily Mail*, all came out in his support. The Free Trade Unionists could count only on *The Spectator*. However, this Press support was not matched by support among the electorate, who still shied away from 'dear food'. Tariff reform split the Unionists and divided the Cabinet. Ritchie, Balfour of Burleigh, and Devonshire, were still staunch Free Traders; Balfour held the balance although veering slightly towards Chamberlain, who stood supported by his son, Austen, and by Halisbury.

Balfour's concern was to hold the Government together and in particular to keep Devonshire, who was President of the Unionist Council. When he finally committed himself it was in such vague terms as to lose both Free Traders and Chamberlain. Balfour declared that colonial preference was eminently desirable, 'but it has not yet come within the sphere of practical politics.' Balfour's tactics drove out Free Traders and on 16 September 1903 Chamberlain himself resigned to fight for fiscal reform from outside the government (85).

CHAMBERLAIN'S RESIGNATION

In 1886 Chamberlain, who looked like Gladstone's natural successor with a position in the country much more broadly based than his master, resigned to fight Gladstone over Home Rule. If it was an attempt to wrest the leadership from the Liberal leader, it failed dismally. Chamberlain the Radical gave place to Chamberlain the Liberal Unionist and by a fairly rapid transformation to Chamberlain the Colonial statesman [doc. 20].

Chamberlain's resignation in 1903 looked as if it might have a similar purpose. He had carried the country to victory in the South African war and his political position was akin to that of co-prime minister with Lord Salisbury. In the country he was widely popular, and after his resignation he mounted a campaign against the Government's policy which put excessive strain upon the new Balfour administration (22 vol. v).

Are there any obvious similarities between the two situations apart from the unique sight of a successful politician twice in a lifetime abandoning his party's government to campaign outside government for party and national support? One important parallel stands out. In 1886 when Chamberlain had been invited to join the Gladstone government he had asked for the post of Colonial Secretary, to be met by

Gladstone's settled conviction that Secretaryships should be reserved for the great families. Chamberlain was fobbed off with the Presidency of the Local Government Board. In his brief tenure of this office his recommendations to Gladstone were ignored. Gladstone in fact made no attempt to woo the great Radical leader and to keep him by his side.

The reverse was true of Salisbury who, as Julian Amery stresses, recognised Chamberlain's quality. The same was true of their personal relationship - they dined frequently at each other's houses. On 11 July 1902, Salisbury resigned. The King sent for Balfour, Salisbury's nephew, and since 1891 the Leader of the Conservative Party in the Commons. Chamberlain had great support among backbenchers and in the country but not with the great families, who preferred another Cecil. It is impossible to think that Chamberlain did not regard himself as a possible candidate, despite his disavowals a year before. Balfour, a philosophic, detached, urbane, chilly man, did not make the same continuous attempt to keep his lines open with Chamberlain that Salisbury had done. Was Balfour underestimating Chamberlain in a way similar to Gladstone? Was Chamberlain's subsequent challenge and resignation related to Balfour's personal and political failure to keep Chamberlain by his side?

In the subsequent Cabinet reshuffle there were remarkably few Chamberlain supporters. In fact 'except for his son, he could not count on a single whole-hearted adherent in the Government' (22, vol. v).

All his political life Chamberlain had been a man with a cause, an attitude to life and politics singularly distasteful to the new Prime Minister. In 1902 Chamberlain had no immediate cause: his seizure on the new cause of imperial preference was to complete his isolation from the Cabinet and to lead him into resignation, and thereafter into an attempt to recreate within the country a sense of political mission.

CHAMBERLAIN'S CONCEPT OF TARIFF REFORM

When Chamberlain resigned, did he have a clear idea of what he intended to fight for? Taxes on imported foodstuffs meant only one thing to the voter: higher food prices. To counter this with the claim of a 'scientific tariff' was to ignore the total lack of information available on the likely effect of food taxes on food prices. Certainly within Chamberlain's scheme preference would be given to colonial produce, thereby drawing the emotional bonds of empire tighter together through easier commerce.

But why restrict taxes on imports to foodstuffs? Chamberlain said he was no Protectionist. Even though support for Tariff Reform was to come from industrialists Chamberlain went no further than Balfour in his attitude to industrial tariffs. Tariffs could be retaliatory, intended to force the foreigner to get rid of his own tariffs to enable British trade to flow freely once more. Beyond this he would only support tariffs to protect the country against the dumping of foreign goods (81).

If the leader of the tariff campaign was himself so unorthodox in his attitude to tariffs, how could it be reasonably expected that such a cause would animate the British public and voter?

Chamberlain's exchanges with the King when he resigned make interesting reading. The King misunderstood Chamberlain's reasons for resigning and in his letter referred to a difference of viewpoint between the government and Chamberlain. Immediately Chamberlain replied pointing out that 'Mr Balfour and his present colleagues agree with Mr Chamberlain.' The difference is not even in timing for Chamberlain recognised that the proposals were 'for the moment politically impracticable.' He resigned because 'it would not be consistent for him to be in a Cabinet whose programme did not include this important item.' It looked as if Chamberlain's faith in his own abilities to win over the country - as he had as a Radical in 1885 - was leading him to take up a position which had more than a mark of absurdity about it. Ritchie and his Free Trade friends had gone. What issue still lay between him and Balfour? Was the contest for different stakes altogether? Lady Frances Balfour wrote: 'I don't see why people think Chamberlain's action is fine. If he wins, he must be the next Prime Minister.'

The irony of the situation is clear. To Free Traders the Government seemed now Protectionist: the arch Protectionist was outside this Government, working, it seemed, for its replacement by his own administration.

THE TARIFF REFORM CAMPAIGN

Chamberlain began what was for his times an unparalleled whistle stop tour in the autumn of 1903 with a major policy speech in Glasgow. This was the first stop in a tour which took him to Newcastle upon Tyne, Tynemouth, Liverpool, Birmingham, Cardiff, Leeds, and the City of London.

One of his major arguments was that trade lost to protectionist countries had been offset by increased trade with the colonies. Colonial trade then was essential to Britain's economic wellbeing. He calculated colonial trade as representing work for 750,000 workers. He then went to dwell on the Empire as 'a splendid sentiment'. 'We must either draw closer together or we shall drift apart' [doc. 22].

At Greenock he argued the case for retaliatory tariffs: 'I am a Free Trader.' 'I want to have exchange with all the nations of the world, but if they will not exchange with me, then I am not a Free Trader at any price.'

Imperial preference, protection where necessary, this is how Chamberlain mounted a campaign which was to produce detailed criticism of Liberals and Free Trade Unionists alike. His speeches were cunningly geared to local economic circumstances in a way to make political friends. In Cardiff, for instance, he invoked the dangers of foreign competition in coal, tinplate and steel.

The success of the campaign might be seen in by-elections. In the first two at Dulwich and Lewisham, both marginal Unionist seats, the candidates at first took the Balfour line but under pressure came out for Chamberlain before the elections on 15 December 1903. Both seats were won for the Government with large majorities. 'The two by-elections exceeded my most sanguine expectations,' commented Chamberlain.

At Leeds Chamberlain announced the setting up of a Tariff Commission (organised by the Tariff Reform League) to collect evidence and to frame policy for 'a scientific tariff'.

How far was Chamberlain's campaign related to the economic realities? Certainly there is general agreement amongst economic historians that the early years of the twentieth century marked a significant change in the state of the British economy in which 'it passed from its remarkable 'late Victorian growth to a condition, by no means stagnant or declining, but showing slower progress' **(74)**. The signs of the change were visible in many ways. The English birthrate had fallen since 1877 and the family of two or at most three children began to be the established pattern. It was Chamberlain who ordered a census of the whole Empire, and in 1906 the figures were published—the Empire had a white population of 54 million (2.3 million less than Germany in 1905). Imperial trade could widen the market for all participants to something like the size of the German or American one.

British sales of her major products, such as cotton goods, linen, woollen and worsted, were at best static and in some cases were declining, and the figures for exports to protected countries were far worse. The list of protectionist countries had grown long, beginning with Germany in 1879, Russia in 1882, Austria and France in 1882. Tariffs were repeatedly being raised. British steel production rose only slowly from 3,579,000 tons in 1890 to 4,901,000 tons in 1900 (the comparable figures for Germany are 2,195,000 to 6,260,000).

Certainly the technological initiative had moved elsewhere, and as

H.J. Habbakuk has shown the conditions of English society militated against English entrepreneurship. 'In the coal industry, in 1913, more than 40 per cent of the American coal output was mechanically cut, as against 8.5 per cent of the British' **(90)**. Labour-saving devices were more readily adopted in America, Germany and Belgium in the steel industry than they were in Britain.

Markets were, perhaps, the key. Germany and America had the economic stimulus of expanding markets, Britain did not. Chamberlain's economic policy was aimed at creating new markets, partly protected, for a country which had industrialised early and had therefore settled into an economic framework which could not change as readily as countries coming late into the race for industrialisation.

CHAMBERLAIN VERSUS BALFOUR

Balfour's strategy in dealing with Chamberlain's resignation had been geared to keeping Devonshire, the most aristocratic of the Liberal Unionists and a Free Trader, in his Cabinet. However, Balfour's own public commitment to tariff reform when practicable led to Devonshire's resignation.

Outside the Government he was still President of the Liberal Unionist Council and therefore able to tell voters not to support candidates whose fiscal views were unsound. Devonshire the Whig and Chamberlain the Radical had been allies since they broke Gladstone's Home Rule Bill in 1886. By tactics reminiscent of his work with the National Liberal Federation Chamberlain ousted Devonshire from the Presidency. At the annual meeting of the Liberal Unionist Council on 18 May 1904 he called for new rules to democratise the Association. Chamberlain became the new President of an Association committed to fiscal reform.

Chamberlain's long term strategy rested on a conviction that the Liberals would win the next election. What he wanted was an immediate dissolution, an election fought on his programme and an eventual acceptance by the electorate of the rightness of his policies during the disastrous course of the ensuing Liberal administration. Balfour, however, was reluctant to hand over power, and almost as reluctant to come out for the full Chamberlain programme.

Chamberlain had proposed that a Colonial Conference should be called to work out the details of a preferential tariff. Balfour was willing to accept this but he insisted there must first be a general election to give a mandate for such a conference and that when a conference had worked out policies there should be a further general election to approve the new policies. It was the doctrine of the referendum in disguise. For Chamberlain the second election was the real stumbling block but, from this position Balfour was never to retreat. Chamberlain's tactics were aimed at stressing the similarities in their approach and suppressing what seemed to him the dangerous proposal for yet another election.

In other ways Chamberlain's position differed from that of Balfour. His speeches took on a mid-twentieth-century turn in their concern for full employment. The old radical reappeared in such passages as: 'I have never been able to see how a rich man would be materially benefited by my policy. . . I think it is possible he might lose more than he would gain. . . but thr question is how to increase the employment of the working classes.' (It was in (**22, vol 6**) the same speech delivered in the East End of London that he also spoke out against the evils of unrestricted immigration, again in a way only too familiar today.)

Furthermore Chamberlain had now come out for an allround tariff of 10 per cent as opposed to Balfour's rather dubious policy of retaliatory tariffs, a 10 per cent tariff to be used 'to lower the cost of living of the poor' and 'to carry forward some of those great social reforms which at the present time we cannot afford'.

Chamberlain was now seventy and anxious for results. In a memorandum drawn up at the beginning of 1905 he estimated that of the 374 Unionists in the House, only twenty-seven were totally opposed to any change at all. Of the others, 174 were hardline preferentialists and the remainder were sympathisers who would be won over if the government made preference its stated policy.

In June 1905 Balfour, speaking at the Albert Hall, moved nearer to Chamberlain's position. He made clear that if it were true that the Unionists were not going to win the next election, he would abandon the double election plan for preferential tariffs. Furthermore he agreed that Preference must be regarded as a matter of extreme urgency (**85**).

The first step must be an election. When would the government resign? According to Julian Amery, Balfour travelled to Windsor with the Chamberlains, and Chamberlain said to him: 'I tell you, Arthur, you will wreck the party if you go on. You should have dissolved two years ago.' To which Balfour rejoined, 'Well, I suppose you are right.' This suggests that Balfour was already inclining towards resignation before at Bristol, at the Liberal Unionists' Council Annual Conference, Chamberlain rejected all compromise within the party: his policy must be accepted, the fainthearts and waverers must go.

On 4 December 1905 Balfour resigned. The differences between Balfour and Chamberlain were still very wide. The election results could not have been more disastrous. The Liberals under Campbell-Bannerman won 377 seats, the Irish 83, and Labour 53. On the Government side Chamberlain's supporters won 109, Balfourites 32, Free Fooders 11— 513 to 157. Only in Birmingham were the results at all heartening. Every constituency returned a Unionist, with increased majorities. Elsewhere even ministers, even the ex-Prime Minister lost their seats.

Why such a landslide? Both Fraser (84) and Amery (22, vol 6) agree that the Labour movement's opposition was a major cause. The Unionist record in social reform was negligible: no major social reform had been carried. Furthermore Chamberlain had made no move to woo the trade union leaders. The fiscal question counted little except in terms of the tragi-comic picture of the Chamberlain-Balfour contests carried out in public and private over the last three years.

One result of this disaster was the Valentine Compact, an attempt to bridge the widening gulf between Balfour and Chamberlain. This was an exchange of letters on St Valentine's Day, 14 February 1906. Again Balfour's concern to hold the party together, and no doubt to retain the leadership, is shown by these letters in which he agreed not only on the immediate need for fiscal reform but also on the establishment of a 'moderate general tariff on manufactured goods' (doc. 23).

Chamberlain had won. His victory in personal terms was shortlived. On 11 July 1906, the day after he had given an exhausting speech at Bingley Hall, Birmingham, he returned to London and attended the meeting of the Tariff Commission, although, as he said to a friend, 'he was a wreck'. In the early evening of the same day he collapsed from a stroke which left him incapacitated until his death in 1914. There had been early warning signs—occasional inability to remember a word when delivering a speech and on one occasion a short time, a very short time, when he was robbed of the power of speech altogether, but nothing as massive as this stroke which paralysed the whole of his right side (84).

PART THREE

Assessment

Assessment

Chamberlain's great gifts, of personality, of intellect, his oratory, all helped to give him control of Birmingham, and almost to give him control of the Liberal Party, the Conservatives and ultimately the country. Yet only in Birmingham was he entirely successful. What finally prevented him reaching that rank which his gifts seemed to merit and his ambition strained after? Was it his extraordinary impulsiveness? or his overvaulting ambition? or should Chamberlain be seen as ultimately handicapped by his class background, the fact that he was not a 'real gentleman' with 'the necessary tact and behaviour' of that caste, and in this sense as much a victim of class prejudice as Richard Cobden in his dealings with the Whig oligarchs? Or does such a view ignore a lack in Chamberlain of that final political tact which enables a politician to decide when best to resign in order to carry most support with him?

Chamberlain's career, judged by any standards except perhaps his own, was quite remarkable, particularly in nineteenth-century terms. On his way from successful Midland screw-manufacturer to Cabinet office, he had a good deal of prejudice to overcome. His experience in Birmingham provided a firm basis for much that followed. Slum clearance, water supplies, the civic gospel, pointed the way to what was needed in the Empire. Even here there is paradox for although as Colonial Secretary he could see the relevance of his Birmingham experience to the West Indies, unrecovered from their mid-century decline, he did not bring to national politics the same concern for the material environment which marked him out as one of Birmingham's most outstanding mayors.

Chamberlain made Birmingham the centre of political life, wresting from Manchester that provincial leadership which the Free Trade movement had given her. His use of central government funds made available by Disraeli's social legislation made Birmingham a model of city improvement and her townscape benefited, if not permanently, at least until the administration of the 1970s rebuilt the city around an inner motorway.

From Birmingham came a doctrine of municipal reform nurtured by

Birmingham nonconformity: from Birmingham, too, came the new form of political organisation which helped to bring within the political pale the newly enfranchised voters of the 1867 Reform Act. The Birmingham Liberal Federation colonised other large provincial towns and created a framework based on firm executive control and local associations. The cry of American-style politics went up, the caucus was seen as a method of non-democratic control from the top. Clearly Schnadhorst and Chamberlain ran the organisation, and their control justified the criticisms made of the National Liberal Federation. What is even more clearly American is the attempt to bring the new voter into politics: in America it was the immigrant and the ward boss and the political machine promising jobs in return for votes. Chamberlain's juggernaut faced a similar problem: how to include within British political life the new political nation which Parliament had created.

When the test came in 1886 the machine failed to follow Chamberlain into opposition. The control his critics claimed he had achieved proved wanting and the Federation largely followed its own political judgment. The organisational model Chamberlain and Birmingham created was adopted by the Conservatives and, much later, the Labour Party. His achievement was to provide a model for organised politics.

Birmingham gave Chamberlain, too, that sensitivity to the economic problems of his time which was not a marked characteristic of the establishment politicians of either of the great parties. He took his Colonial Secretaryship at a time when Birmingham and Britain were losing the great economic advantage that early industrialisation had achieved. Germany and the United States were more rapidly expanding production and their economies, and Chamberlain came to see that orthodox Liberal doctrine had little relevance for Britain as a whole and for the Black Country in particular. From the platform at Bingley Hall he thundered out his proposals for improvement, with industries protected against competition and a rightful market established within the Empire. His speeches and his correspondence give evidence of a barometric sensitivity to business discontents, and from Birmingham he was more closely in contact with economic realities than was Salisbury at Hatfield. Highbury may have been in salubrious Edgbaston but Aston, Walsall and Dudley were not far distant. The proposals he worked out for imperial Free Trade and then for Imperial Preference turned on the need of Britain rather than the problems of the self-governing colonies. His claim 'there are many things which you do not make, many things for which we have a great capacity of production. Leave them to us as you have left them hitherto', was directed inwards to Britain's necessities rather than outwards towards the colonies themselves.

Here as elsewhere, Chamberlain often seemed to be the victim of his own euphoric platform displays, reluctant to see the strength of his opponents' case, and even the weakness of his own (56). R.V. Kubicek, in his study of Chamberlain at the Colonial Office, cites one outstanding example of this characteristic in Chamberlain. On the eve of Devonshire's resignation in 1903, Chamberlain wrote to his old ally accusing him of 'indifference to a great policy' and yet inconsequently in the same letter charging Devonshire with straining at 'my gnat'.

As a politician Chamberlain was clearly swayed by deeply felt social compassion for the disadvantaged of his time. His work in Birmingham, the Radical Programme itself, his concept of 'ransom', all point to the extent of that sympathy. As a Liberal, it is arguable, he was never in a political position where he could translate into practical terms his own vision of an improvement scheme for the whole of society, with the exception of his support for the 1884 Reform Act. As a member of a Conservative government and for so long effectively co-Prime Minister, this argument is more difficult to advance. Faced by the splendid panorama of Empire, social reforms such as old age pensions lost their urgency, gave way in fact to large schemes which might in the long term raise the general standard of life in Britain, but the long term was obviously very long indeed.

At two major points in his career Chamberlain split the party of which he was a member. First, he opposed the revered Gladstone over Home Rule: second, he divided Conservatives and Liberal Unionists on the question of the Tariff Reform. Is this the action of a leader given to impulsive action, resigning from governments which had clear majorities in the House, or is this the action of a politician forced on by political principle? Is it a question of a disappointed politician robbed of the Colonial Office in the first instance, and deprived of an even greater prize in the second? Resigning not in pique, or on principle, but as part of a calculated move to bring down the leader of the party – a Gladstone who had offended the Whigs and Radicals and was unlikely to get the support of the nation, and a Balfour who had inherited a mantle which might well be wrested from him? Is it indicative of a final lack of political insight that both these major political actions failed of their objectives? The first put the Liberals out of office for six years while still retaining Gladstone in the leadership: the second sent a divided party to the polls in 1905.

Even if Chamberlain's actions are interpreted in the most favourable way as decisions forced on him not by ambition—and it would be legitimate for him to feel the slight on both occasions—but by his own assessment of political realities, nevertheless both actions cast doubt on his political judgment. Within the framework of the Kilmainham Treaty the Irish Party in the House was committed to a solution of the Irish problem in constitutional terms: no ultimate good could come of an attempt to thwart the limited political objective which the Home Rule Bill promised to the Irish. Better by far to leave the odium of rejection to the Lords. Again the Irish Party could muster something like eighty-six M.P.s in the House, and these were at the disposal of Gladstone after his 'conversion' and were to remain at the disposal of the Liberals until 1914. To cast off these safe votes in the Commons for the sake of differences between the Central Board Scheme and Home Rule which were barely visible to the naked eye seemed unbelievably shortsighted.

The justification for the second resignation seems even slimmer than the first. It was easy to whip up popular feeling on Ireland, to count on Ulster, to conjure up a vision of an Empire falling into ruins through his steady advance of Home Rule. Less easy to create a commitment to Tariff Reform. For the businessman feeling the chill of competition, Chamberlain, by extending his campaign from imperial preference to tariff reform was talking a language for which he had an instinctive sympathy. For the Liberal and for many Liberal Unionists, for many Conservatives, brought up on the doctrine of Free Trade, Chamberlain's policy represented not only a move from established principle but a move into the unknown. Free Trade had made the country great. What sense was there in abandoning it? What basis could there be in the country or in the House for a policy which was either anathema or incomprehensible unless put into impossibly simple terms? Chamberlain has seriously overestimated the appeal of his programme to a working-class electorate. The electoral defeat of 1905, with 400 Liberals opposing 157 Conservative and Unionists, gave a clear answer to the Chamberlain campaign. Of this diminished party in the House, perhaps two-thirds supported Chamberlain, and Balfour was taking on the appearance of a party leader on the point of resignation. However, Chamberlain did not push his advantage and the Valentine letters set the seal on the agreement to make tariff reform the 'first constructive work of the Unionist Party'. The Opposition had a new policy, for what might be a very distant future.

Within the Empire also his record is equivocal. The great concepts of the Colonial Conferences ran up against the determined national self-interests of the colonies themselves. An Imperial Council looked attractive to Chamberlain and his imperialist friends: to Canadian statesmen it looked more like a way of reducing their hard won indepence. From the Conferences little came out except the idea of Imperial Preference. In the event his support for research in tropical medicine and his attempts to involve business interests in colonial development must rank amongst his successes. In South Africa, his own policy, relatively cautious and restrained, was defeated by his own High Commissioner, Milner, who first advocated reform or war but rapidly concentrated on war as the appropriate tactic to advance imperial interests in South Africa. Milner's handling of the Bloemfontein conference was in line with Milner's own views, and not Chamberlain's, and the Colonial Secretary's insistence that his negotiator should 'lay all stress on the question of the franchise, was disregarded. The South African war secured its objective. It united South Africa under British leadership but the war itself and the revelation of the concentration camps had helped to deflate the balloon of imperialism.

Ultimately it is possible to see the Imperial Economic Conference in Ottowa in 1932 and the acceptance of imperial preference as a fulfilment of Chamberlain's dream, but this was no basis for imperial unity—no more than shelter in the economic blizzard. Chamberlain's achievements, great at the local and personal level, seem slight at the level of national politics. A successful business man, influential civic leader, an astute political organiser, a commanding public speaker and a politician who gave prestige to what was once a minor office—this was Joseph Chamberlain of Birmingham.

PART FOUR

Documents

The New Radicalism — I

Joseph Chamberlain on the Church of England, speaking at Manchester Free Trade Hall, 22 January 1872

The Bishop of Manchester, whose outspoken utterances we admire, even when we most differ from him, told us the other day that the clergy were like other men, actuated with similar motives, and with the same feelings, and the same virtues. I willingly believe it, and when, therefore, I see them as a body always opposed to the popular side, always on the side of property and privilege, I say the fault cannot be in the men, it must be in the system. I say the differences must not be sought in the differences of religion, or in human nature; it must be sought, and will be found, in that peculiar institution which renders the clergy of our Established Church out of time and out of harmony with the aspirations of a free people.

(4, i. 14).

The New Radicalism — II

Joseph Chamberlain on education speaking at Severn Street School, Birmingham, 30 November 1874

It seems to me that education must be a perfect farce when the instruction at the school is contradicted by the experience at home. It seems to me absurd to preach morality to people who are herded together in conditions in which common decency is impossible. It seems to me ridiculous to talk of temperance to men who have every reason to leave their homes, and are driven thereby to the public-house. It seems to me monstrous to preach thrift to those whose lives are wasted in a perpetual struggle with disease and death.

(4, i. 5).

The New Radicalism — III

Joseph Chamberlain explaining why he is a Radical in a speech at Birmingham, 12 October 1874

I am a Radical Reformer because I would reform and remove ignorance, poverty, intemperance, and crime at their very roots. What is the cause of all this ignorance and vice? Many people say that intemperance is at the bottom of everything and I am not inclined to disagree with them. I believe we hardly ever find misery or poverty without finding that intemperance is one of the factors in such conditions. But at the same time I believe intemperance itself is only an effect produced by causes that lie deeper still. I should say these causes, in the first place, are the gross ignorance of the masses; and, in the second place, the horrible, shameful homes in which many of the poor are forced to live.

(4, i, 43).

Plain Words to Peers, Denbigh, 20 October 1884.

Chamberlain prepares for battle with the Lords over the 1884 Franchise Bill, which the Lords were threatening to block unless it were linked with a redistribution Bill.

Are the Lords to dictate to us, the people of England? Are the Lords to dictate to us the laws which we shall make and the way in which we shall bring them in? Are you going to be governed by yourselves? Or will you submit to an oligarchy which is a mere accident of birth? . . . The chronicles of the House of Lords are one long record of concessions delayed until they have lost their grace, of rights denied until extorted from their fears. It has been a history of one long contest between the representatives of privilege and the representatives of popular rights, and during this time the Lords have perverted, delayed, and denied justice until at last they gave grudgingly and churlishly what they could no longer withhold.

(5, p. 95)

Ransom for property?

This is the doctrine of 'ransom' which so alarmed the propertied classes.

But then I ask, what ransom will property pay for the security which it enjoys? What substitute will it find for the natural rights which have ceased to be recognised? Society is banded together in order to protect itself against the instincts of those of its members who would make very short work of private ownership if they were left alone. That is all very well, but I maintain that society owes these men something more than mere toleration in return for the restrictions which it places upon their liberty of action.

Speech at Birmingham, 5 January 1885 **(4)**.

The Radical diagnosis

I believe that the great difficulty with which we have to deal is the excessive inequality in the distribution of riches. Ignorance, intemperance, immorality and disease — these things are all interdependent and closely connected; and although they are often the cause of poverty, they are still more frequently the cause of destitution . . . It is not our duty, it is not our wish, to pull down and abase the rich, although I do not think that the excessive aggregation of wealth in a few hands is any advantage to anybody; but our object is to raise the general condition of the people.

Speech at Hull, 5 August 1885 **(4)**.

The State of the Nation

Politics is the science of human happiness, and the business of a statesman and of politicians is to find out how they can raise the general condition of the people; how they can increase the happiness of those who are less fortunate among them. What are the facts of the case? I sometimes think that we are so used to poverty and to its consequences that we forget it or neglect it. Yet surely there is some reason to doubt the perfection of our system when in this, the richest country in the world, one in thirty of the population at every moment are unable to obtain the means of subsistence without recourse to the parish, and one in ten at the same time are on the verge of starvation.

Speech at Glasgow, 15 September 1885 (4).

document 8

Chamberlain's Central Board Scheme

The plan which has been forming itself in my mind for some time past is to have a thoroughly effective popular county government on the same lines and with the same powers as that proposed for England and Scotland, and then to complete the work by establishing a central board consisting either of delegates from the county boards or of separately elected representatives to whom might be entrusted the full control of such questions as are dealt with now in Ireland by the local government board, the board of works, the board of education and other similar bodies.

Chamberlain to Morley, 21 January 1885 (37).

document 9

The National Council scheme as set out in the Radical Programme

In administering the affairs of any county it would soon be seen that there are many matters in which the co-operation of other counties might be required, and for the accomplishment of which it would be necessary to impose taxes over an area wider than that of a single county, or even to assess a national rate. This necessity proves that in addition to the County

Boards bodies of national authority and jurisdiction must be called into existence. Of these bodies, which for sake of convenience we have called National Councils, one might sit in Edinburgh, one in Dublin, and if the people of Wales desire it, one should be established in Wales.

The establishment of a National Council, elected by the Irish people and endowed with national authority, would enable the Imperial Parliament to delegate to a body of sufficient weight, capacity, and power duties which Parliament now endeavours to perform, but the performance of which necessitates the neglect of other and more important matters upon which the attention of the great legislative assembly of the Empire should be concentrated.

Extract from 'Local Government and Ireland', (28, pp. 249, 250).

document 10

Chamberlain and Ulster

If, to begin with, the representation of Ireland at Westminster were maintained on its present footing — if Irishmen were allowed to vote and to speak on all subjects which were not specially referred to them at Dublin, then they would remain an integral part of this Imperial realm; they would have their share in its privileges, and their responsibility for its burdens. In that case the Imperial Parliament would be able to maintain its control over Imperial taxation in Ireland, and for all Imperial purposes the Parliament at Westminster would speak for a United Kingdom. I should like to see the case of Ulster met in some form or other. I would be glad if it were found possible to concede to Ulster, having regard to the great distinctions which I have pointed out of race, and religion, and politics — I would be glad if there could be conceded to Ulster a separate assembly.

Speech at the Town Hall, Birmingham, 21 April 1886 (4, i. 271).

Chamberlain in Gladstone's Third Ministry, 1886

Chamberlain recorded his interview with Gladstone, when he expressed a preference for the Colonial Office. In the event he was appointed President of the Local Government Board.

On January 31 [1886] I asked him to see me again as to the office I was to hold. I explained my objections to taking the control of one of the great spending and military departments. He then asked me what office I would prefer. I mentioned the Colonial Office, but, at the same time, told him that I would not allow this question to interfere and if it were not convenient to him to make another arrangement I would take the First Lordship or any other office he liked to offer. He made no reply to my suggestion of the Colonial Office but asked me whether I would go back to the Board of Trade.

(**26**, p. 188)

Resignation

I gathered from your statements that although your plans are not finally matured, yet that you have come to the conclusion that any extension of local government on municipal lines, including even the creation of a National Council or Councils for purely Irish business, would now be entirely inadequate; and that you are convinced of the necessity for conceding a separate legislative Assembly for Ireland with full powers to deal with all Irish affairs. . . .

My public utterances and my conscientious convictions are absolutely opposed to such a policy and I feel that the differences which have now been disclosed are so vital that I can no longer entertain the hope of being of service in the Government. . . .

Extract from Chamberlain's letter of resignation, 15 March 1886 (**26**, p. 195).

Chamberlain on Gladstone's Home Rule Bill

Record of an interview between R.B. O'Brien and Joseph Chamberlain.

Mr Chamberlain. 'I was never near being converted to an Irish Parliament. The national councils was my extreme point. There I stood.'

'I should like to talk to you about what you said on the subject of Canadian Home Rule. I am satisfied that you attacked the exclusion of the Irish members to kill the Bill, but I think you said things about Canada which are open to the interpretation that you might favour the establishment of an Irish Parliament. The matter is not quite clear to me.'

Mr Chamberlain. 'I do not think you should press me too hard. I stated my object was to kill the Bill. I have no doubt I said many things that may have been open to some such interpretation as you suggest. . . However open I may be to criticism in whatever I said, my aim, was, as I say, to kill the Bill.'

(**92** p. 141)

Kruger and the Uitlanders

President Kruger, at the Bloemfontein Conference, 1899, explains the basis of his opposition to the enfranchisement of the Uitlanders.

Our enfranchised burghers are probably about 30,000, and the newcomers may be from 60,000 to 70,000; and if we give them the franchise tomorrow, we may as well give up the republic. I hope you will clearly see that I shall not get it through with my people.

CO 417/26, quoted in (**23**, p. 180).

Chamberlain on British policy towards the Transvaal

If H.M. Govt should decide to send an ultimatum, what should they ask for? It seems difficult to treat as *casus belli* refusal by state to which we have given complete internal independence to grant a particular form of franchise to aliens. Yet we must ask for something definite which will meet the existing situation.

What do you think of the following? 'The repeal of all legislation since the Convention of 1884 restrictive of the rights and privileges enjoyed by aliens when the Convention was arranged.'

Chamberlain to Milner, telegram, 7 June 1899, CO 417/279, quoted in (23, p. 181).

A question of expediency

Our despatch reviewing the situation and stating latest conditions of settlement can be sent by telegraph in a few days or delayed indefinitely as may be most expedient.

The advantage of delay is that we shall gain time for arrival of reinforcements; and also that we shall not have disclosed our hand. The disadvantage is that we may again be entangled in negotiations about five, six or seven years' franchise or other details which will cause delay, alienate our friends, encourage opposition in this country, and after all lead to no permanent settlement. If Boers were to make new offer, before presentation of ultimatum, it would be almost impossible to refuse consideration, and I have now lost hope of a real settlement on the lines of your Bloemfontein proposals.

If, however, presentation of new proposals were to precipitate a conflict and your military advisers think that there would be substantial risks political considerations must give way to military exigencies.

The question is, can you hold your own till reinforcements arrive? If so, it is not our policy to do anything to encourage efforts of Free State or others to delay offensive proceedings on the part of the Boers.

All this is on the assumption that Kruger will certainly not make concessions sufficient to ensure a lasting peace and render unnecessary the permanent maintenance of a large force in South Africa. Otherwise, of course, I would still preach patience.

But if war is inevitable it is best for us that the Boers should begin it.

Chamberlain to Milner, 2 October 1899, CO 417/267, quoted in (**23**, pp. 201-2).

document 17

The imperial vision

The position of this country is not one without anxiety to statesmen and careful observers. The political jealousy of which I have spoken, the commercial rivalry more serious than anything we have yet had, the pressure of hostile tariffs, the pressure of bounties, the pressure of subsidies, it is all becoming more weighty and more apparent. What is the object of this system adopted by countries which, at all events, are very prosperous themselves – countries like Germany and other large Continental States? What is the object of this policy of bounties and subsidies? It is admitted; there is no secret about it; the intention is to shut out this country, as far as possible, from all profitable trade with those foreign States and, at the same time, to enable those foreign States to undersell us in British markets. That is the policy; and we see that it is assuming a great development, that old ideas of trade and free competition have changed. We are face to face with great combinations, with enormous trusts, having behind them gigantic wealth. Even the industries and commerce which we thought to be peculiarly our own, even those are in danger. It is quite impossible that these new methods of competition can be met by adherence to old and antiquated methods which were perfectly right at the time at which they were developed. At the present moment, the Empire is being attacked on all sides and, in our isolation, we must look to ourselves. We must draw closer our internal relations, the ties of sentiment, the ties of sympathy, yes, and the ties of interest. If by adherence to economic pedantry, to old shibboleths, we are to lose opportunities of closer union which are offered us by our colonies, if we are to put aside occasions now within our grasp, if we do not take every chance in our power to keep British trade in British hands, I am certain that we shall deserve the disasters which will infallibly come upon us.

. . . The days are for great Empires and not for little States. . . .

Chamberlain speaking at Birmingham Town Hall, 16 May 1902, quoted in (22, iv, 405).

document 18
A policy for Empire

If we choose the Empire might be self-sustaining; it is so wide, its products are so various; its climates so different that there is absolutely nothing which is necessary to our existence, hardly. anything which is desirable as a luxury which cannot be produced within the boundaries of the Empire itself.

But the Empire at the present time, and especially the United Kingdom which is the greatest market of the world – derives the greatest part of its necessaries from foreign countries, and exports the largest part of its available . . . produce also to foreign countries. . . . Now, I confess, that to my mind, that is not a satisfactory state of things and I hope you will agree with me that everything which can possibly tend to increase the interchange of products between the different parts of the Empire is deserving of our cordial encouragement.

From Chamberlain's opening speech to the Colonial Conference, 1902, quoted in (22, v, 45).

document 19
Decisions of the Colonial Conference, 1902

1. That this Conference recognises that the principle of preferential trade between the United Kingdom and His

Majesty's Dominions beyond the Seas would stimulate and facilitate mutual commercial intercourse, and would, by promoting the development of the resources and industries of the several parts, strengthen the Empire.

2. That this Conference recognises that, in the present circumstances of the Colonies, it is not practicable to adopt a general stystem of Free Trade as between the Mother Country and the British Dominions beyond the Seas.

3. That with a view, however, to promoting the increase of trade within the Empire, it is desirable that those Colonies which have not already adopted such a policy should, as far as their circumstances permit, give substantial preferential treatment to the products and manufactures of the United Kingdom.

4. That the Prime Ministers of the Colonies respectfully urge on His Majesty's Government the expediency of granting in the United Kingdom preferential treatment to the products and manufactures of the Colonies either by exemption from or reduction of duties now or hereafter imposed.

5. That the Prime Ministers present at the Conference undertake to submit to their respective Governments at the earliest opportunity the principle of the resolution and to request them to take such measures as may be necessary to give effect to it.

A covering memorandum warned:

The Canadian Ministers desired to have it understood that they took this course [of submitting the resolution] with the strong hope and expectation that the principle of preferential trade would be more widely accepted by the Colonies, and that the Mother Country would, at an early date, apply the same principle by exempting the products of the Colonies from Customs duties.

If, after using every effort to bring about such a readjustment of the fiscal policy of the Empire, the Canadian Government should find that the principle of preferential trade is not acceptable to the Colonies generally or the Mother Country, then Canada should be free to take such action as might be deemed necessary in the presence of such conditions.

Minutes of the Conference and covering Memorandum, quoted in (**22**, v, 54).

The imperial vision and the new Empire.

I have felt for some time that this is a critical period in the history of the Empire. What we do now and what our colonies do will probably in the course of the earlier years of this century settle for all time the question whether a new Empire, such as has never entered into the conception of man before — an Empire bound together by invisible ties and yet of extraordinary strength — whether such an Empire shall be consolidated and maintained or whether we are to drop apart into several atoms, each caring only for our local and parochial interests. The Imperial idea has only recently taken root in this country. We have only to look back to the lifetime of many of us to remember a period of apathy and indifference, in which our statesmen were eager chiefly to rid themselves of responsibility, and felt that home affairs were as much as they could properly be called upon to attend to. At that time our colonies were crying in vain for our sympathy. Now we have gone ahead; now, I think, we are perhaps, even in advance of our colonies. Not, indeed, that there is on their part, as I have had sufficient testimony, any indifference to the common interest, any want of feeling or affection; but that their own local affairs have become so important and so absorbing that, perhaps, they have failed to appreciate adequately all that is due from them as members of the Empire to which they are proud to belong. The old idea of dominion was an authority to be used by the central State for its own advantages. The new conception of Empire is of a voluntary organisation based on community of interests and community of sacrifices, to which all should bring their contribution to the common good. It is this new spirit, I believe, which we have need to infuse into our colonies. Our kinsfolk may be educated to this great ideal, but the gospel must be preached from colonial pulpits. It is not enough to lecture our children in addresses from home. Missionaries of Empire must spread the faith by personal intercession. Rome was not built in a day. A great Empire on novel principles is not to be consolidated and established in days, or months, or years; but we may be encouraged by the past to look forward to the future. Who is there among us who a few years ago would have ventured to predict that in a time of stress and difficulty the colonies would one and all

— those even who were only indirectly interested — have leapt to our assistance, would have made sacrifices immense so far as they are personal, in so far as they are pecuniary, notable? If that should have happened in so short a course of time, what may we not expect in the future? We ourselves are true to this great and inspiring mission. We have faith in the future, and are prepared to make the sacrifices in which we call upon others to join. My Lord Mayor, I think this object is so important that I am hoping, despite the criticism to which I have referred, you may find in the future worse employment for your Secretaries of State than to send them tramping over the globe in order to preach the doctrine of the Imperial mission of the British Empire.

Chamberlain, speaking at Guildhall, London, 20 March 1903, quoted in (**22**, v, 148).

document 21

The Empire as a trading relation

It seems to me not at all an impossible assumption that before the end of this present century we may find our fellow subjects beyond the seas as numerous as we are at home. I want you to look forward. I want you to consider the infinite importance of this not only to yourselves but to your descendants. Now is the time when you can exert influence. Do you wish that if these ten millions become forty millions they shall still be closely, intimately, affectionately, united to you, or do you contemplate the possibility of their being separated, going off each in his own direction, under a separate flag? Think what it means to your power and influence as a country; think what it means to your position among the nations of the world; think what it means to your trade and commerce — I put that last. The influence of the Empire is the thing I think most about, and that influence, I believe, will always be used for the peace and civilisation of the world.

But the question of trade and commerce is of the greatest importance. Unless that is satisfactorily settled, I for one do not believe in a continued union of the Empire. I hear it stated again and again by what I believe to be the represent-atives of a small minority of the people of this country, those

95

whom I describe, because I know no other words for them, as 'Little Englanders' — I hear it stated by them, what is a fact, that our trade with those countries is much less than our trade with foreign countries, and therefore it appears to be their opinion that we should do everything in our power to cultivate that trade with foreigners, and that we can safely disregard the trade with our children.

That is not my conclusion. My conclusion is exactly the opposite. To look into the future, I say that is the business of British tradesmen to do everything they can, even at some present sacrifice, to keep the trade of the Colonies with Great Britain, to increase the trade and promote it, even if in doing so we lessen somewhat the trade with our foreign competitors.

Chamberlain speaking at Birmingham, 15 May 1903, in (4, i, 130-1).

The value of Empire

I ask you to remember that the future of this country, which we all cherish so much, lies in the future of the British race. The Colonies and possession — they are the natural buttresses of our Imperial state, and it behoves us to think of them as they are now, in their youth and promise, to think of them also as they will be a century hence when grown to manhood and developing beyond anything we can hope for their motherland. Think of them as they are; think of them as they will be; share and sympathize with their aspirations for a closer union: do nothing to discourage them, but show your willingness to cooperate with them in every effort they make or propose. So, and so only, can you maintain the traditions of the past, the renown of this Imperial City, and the permanence of that potent agency for peace and for civilization that we call the British Empire.

Chamberlain, speaking at Guildhall, London, 19 January 1904, quoted in (22, vi, 540).

A political marriage

The letters of 14 February 1906 from which these extracts are taken were published in the morning papers of 15 February. The exchange came to be known as the Valentine Compact.

Balfour to Chamberlain, 14 February 1906: I hold that Fiscal Reform is, and must remain, the first constructive work of the Unionist Party; that the objects of such reform are to secure more equal terms of competition for British trade, and closer commercial union with the Colonies;

that, while it is at present unnecessary to prescribe the exact methods by which these objects are to be attained, and inexpedient to permit differences of opinion as to those methods to divide the Party, . . . though other means may be possible, the establishment of a moderate general tariff on manufactured goods, not imposed for the purpose of raising prices or giving artificial protection against legitimate competition, and the imposition of a small duty on foreign corn, are not in principle objectionable . . .

Chamberlain to Balfour [same day] : . . . I entirely agree with your description of the objects which we both have in view . . .
Quoted in (**22**, vi, 847).

Bibliography

ARTICLES AND SPEECHES BY JOSEPH CHAMBERLAIN
1   a) 'A new political organisation', *Fortnightly Review,* July 1877
     b) 'The Caucus', *Fortnightly Review,* November 1878
2   'A Radical view of the Irish crisis', *Fortnightly Review,* February 1886
3   'The case against Home Rule', *Pall Mall Gazette,* August 1893
4   *Mr. Chamberlain's Speeches,* ed. C.W. Boyd, 2 vols, 1914
5   *Speeches of the Right Hon. Joseph Chamberlain,* ed. H.W. Lang, Routledge, 1885 (Includes 'The Radical Programme')

MANUSCRIPT DOCUMENTS
6   Chamberlain Papers, Birmingham University.

BIRMINGHAM AND CHAMBERLAIN IN MUNICIPAL POLITICS
7   Briggs, Asa. *History of Birmingham,* Oxford University Press, 1952, vol. ii.
8   Allen, G.C. *The Industrial Development of Birmingham and the Journal of the History of Ideas,* ix, 1948
9   Timmins, S. *The Resources, Products and Industrial History of Birmingham and the Midland Hardware District,* London, 1866
10   Dolman, F. 'Joseph Chamberlain's municipal career', *Fortnightly Review,* 1895

THE STRUCTURE OF POLITICS
11   Hanham, H.J. *Elections and Party Management,* Longmans, 1959
12   Vincent, J. *The Formation of the Liberal Party 1857-68,* Constable, 1966
13   Southgate, D. *The Passing of the Whigs,* Macmillan, 1962.
14   Herrick, F.H. 'The second reform movement in Britain, 1850-65', *Journal of the History of Ideas,* ix, 1948.
15   Tholfsen, T.R. 'The transition of democracy in Victorian England', *International Review of Social History,* vi, 1961
16   Smith, F.B. *The Making of the Second Reform Bill,* Cambridge University Press, 1966

17 Herrick, F.H. 'The Reform Bill of 1867 and the British party system', *Pacific Historical Review,* cxi or iii, 1934.
18 Vincent, J.R. 'The effect of the second Reform Act in Lancashire', *Historical Journal,* xi, no. 1, 1968.

CHAMBERLAIN AS POLITICIAN
19 Jenkins, Roy. *Sir Charles Dilke: a Victorian tragedy,* Collins. 1958.
20 Ramm, A, ed. *The Political Correspondence of Mr Gladstone and Lord Granville 1876-1886,* Oxford University Press, 1962.
21 Lloyd, T. *The General Election of 1880,* Oxford University Press, 1968.
22 Garvin, J.L. *Life of Joseph Chamberlain: I. Chamberlain and Democracy, 1836-1885;* II *Disruption and Combat 1885-1895: III. Empire and World Policy 1895-1900;*
Completed by: Amery, Julian. IV. *At the Height of his Powers 1901-3;* V & VI. *Joseph Chamberlain and the Tariff Reform Campaign,* Macmillan, 1934-69.
23 Fraser, P. *Joseph Chamberlain,* Cassell, 1966.
24 Gulley, Elsie C. *Joseph Chamberlain and English Social Politics,* Columbia University Press, 1926.
25 Hurst, M.C. *Joseph Chamberlain and West Midland Politics 1886-1895,* Dugdale Society Oxford, 1962.
26 Chamberlain J. *A Political Memoir* 1880-1892, ed. C.H.D. Howard, Batchworth Press, 1953.
27 Howard, C.H.D. 'Joseph Chamberlain and the Unauthorised Programme', *English Historical Review,* 1xv, 1950.
28 *The Radical Programme, with a preface by J. Chamberlain,* 1885, reprinted 1971, Harvester Press, ed. D. Hamer.
29 Maccoby, S. *English Radicalism 1853-86,* Allen & Unwin, 1935-1961.

THE NATIONAL LIBERAL FEDERATION
30 Herrick, F.H. 'Origins of the National Liberal Federation', *Journal of Modern History,* xvii, 1945.
31 Pelling, Henry. *America and the British Left,* A & C. Black, 1956
32 Shannon, R.J. *Gladstone and the Bulgarian Agitation,* Nelson, 1963.
33 Kelly, Robert. 'Midlothian', *Victorian Studies,* December 1960.
34 McGill, Barry. 'Francis Schnadhorst and Liberal Party organisation', *Journal of Modern History,* March 1962.

35 Tholfsen, 'The Origins of the Birmingham Caucus', *Historical Journal, ii, no.2, 1959.*
36 Watson, R. Spence. *The National Liberal Federation,* London, 1907.

CHAMBERLAIN'S ATTITUDE TO IRELAND
37 Howard, C.H.D. 'Joseph Chamberlain and the Irish "centralboard" scheme', *Irish Historical Studies,* viii, 1952-53.
38 Howard, C.H.D. 'Documents relating to the Irish "central board" scheme 1884-5', *Irish Historical Studies,* viii, 1952-53.
39 Curtis, L.P. *Coercion and Conciliation in Ireland* 1880-92, Princeton University Press, 1963.
40 O'Brien, C.C. *Parnell and his Party 1880-90,* Oxford University Press, 1957.
41 Magnus, Sir P. *Gladstone,* Murray, 1954.
42 Hammond, J.L. *Gladstone and the Irish Nation,* Longmans, 1938.
43 Morley, J. *Life of Gladstone,* 3 vols, London, 1903

IMPERIALISM AND JOSEPH CHAMBERLAIN
44 Bodelsen, C.A. *Studies in Mid-Victorian Imperialism,* Heinemann, 1960.
45 *Cambridge History of the British Empire,* vol. vii.
46 Robinson, R.E. and Gallagher, J. *Africa and the Victorians,* Macmillan, 1963.
47 Thornton, A.P. (a) *The Imperial Idea and its Enemies,* Macmillan, 1959; (b) *Doctrines of Imperialism,* Wiley, 1965.
48 Strauss, W. 'Joseph Chamberlain and the theory of Imperialism', *Public Affairs,* 1942.
49 Koebner, R. 'The Concept of Economic Imperialism', *Economic History Review,* 2nd ser. 11, No. 1, 1-29.
50 Kemp, T. *Theories of Imperialism* 1968, Dobson 1967.
51 Froude, J.A. *Oceana,* 1886.
52 Lockhart, J.G. and Woodhouse, C.M. *Cecil Rhodes,* Hodder & Stoughton, 1962.
53 Cramb, J.A. *Origins and Destiny of Imperial Britain,* Murray, 1935.
54 Dugdale, Blanche. *Arthur James Balfour,* Hutchinson, 1936.
55 Judd, Denis. *Balfour and the British Empire,* Macmillan, 1968.
56 Kubiçek, Robert V. *The Administration of Imperialism: Joseph Chamberlain at the Colonial Office,* Duke University Press, 1969.
57 Kendle, J.E. *The Colonial and Imperial Conferences 1887-1911,* Longmans, 1967.

58   Hobson, J.A. *Imperialism, a Study,* London, 1902.
59   Dunnett, R.E. 'The Campaign against Malaria and the Expansion of scientific, medical and sanitary services in British West Africa, 1898-1910,' *African Historical Studies,* i (1968)
60   Saul, S.B. 'The economic significance of 'Constructive Imperialism', *Journal of Economic History,* xvii, June 1957.
61   Gallagher, J. and Robinson, R. 'The imperialism of Free Trade' *Economic History Review,* 2nd ser., 1953.
62   Seeley, J.E. *The Expansion of England,* London, 1918.

CHAMBERLAIN'S INVOLVEMENT IN SOUTH AFRICA
63   Marais, J.S. *The Fall of Kruger's Republic,* Oxford University Press, 1961.
64   Pakenham, E. *Jameson's Raid,* Weidenfeld & Nicolson, 1960.
65   van der Poel, Jean. *The Jameson Raid,* Capetown, 1951.
66   Drus, E. 'Select documents concerning Anglo-Transvaal Relations 1896-99', *Bulletin of the Institute of Historical Research,* xxvii, 1954.
67   Drus, E. 'Question of imperial complicity in the Jameson Raid' *English Historical Review,* October 1953.
68   Wilde, R.H. 'Joseph Chamberlain and the South African Republic 1895-99', *Archives Year Book for South African History,* i, 1956, (Capetown)
69   Curtis, L.G. *With Curtis in South Africa* Oxford, Blackwell, 1951.
70   Wrench, J.E. *Milner,* Eyre & Spottiswoode, 1958
71   Stokes, Eric. 'Milnerism', *Historical Journal,* vi, 1962
72   Blainey, G. 'Lost causes of the Jameson Raid', *Economic History Review,* 1965.
73   Drus, E. 'A report on the Papers of Joseph Chamberlain relating to the Jameson Raid and the Inquiry', *Bulletin of the Institute of Historical Research,* xxv, 1952.

TARIFF REFORM
74   Ashworth, W. *An Economic History of England 1870-1939,* Methuen, 1960.
75   Sayers, R.S. *History of Economic Change in England 1880-1939,* Oxford University Press 1967.
76   Tyler, J.E. *The Struggle for Imperial Unity 1868-95,* Longmans, 1938.
77   Zebel, G.H. 'Fair trade', *Journal of Modern History,* xii, 1940.
78   MacGoun, A. *A Revenue Tariff within the Empire,* London, 1904.
79   Parkin, G.R. *Imperial Federation,* London, 1892.

80 Holland, Bernard. *Life of the Duke of Devonshire*, 2 vols, Longmans, 1911.
81 Brown, B.R. *The Tariff Reform Movement in Great Britain (1881-95)*, New York, AMS Press, 1943.
82 Hewins, W.A.S. *Apologia of an Imperialist*, 2 vols, Constable, 1929.
83 Hicks Beach, Lady Victoria. *Life of Hicks Beach*, 2 vols, Macmillan, 1932.

CRISIS OF 1905-06
84 Fraser, Peter, 'Unionism and Tariff Reform: the crisis of 1906', *Historical Journal*, v, no.2, 1962.
85 Collin, A.M. *Balfour's Burden*, Blond, 1964.
86 Peel, A.G.V. *The Tariff Reformers*, 1913.

1911
87 Chamberlain, Austen. *Politics from Inside*, Cassell, 1936.
88 Fraser, Peter. 'The Unionist debacle of 1911 and Mr Balfour's retirement', *Journal of Modern History*, December 1963.
89 Jenkins, Roy, *Mr Balfour's Poodle*, Collins, 1954.
90 Habbakuk, H.J. *American & British Technology in the nineteenth century*, Cambridge University Press, 1962.
91 Lloyd, Trevor. *The General Election of 1880*, Oxford University Press, 1968.
92 O'Brien R.B. *Life of C.S. Parnell*, Smith, Elder, 1899.
93 Schoyen, A.R. *The Chartist Challenge*, Heinemann, 1958.
94 Taylor, A.J.P. *The Trouble Makers*, Hamish Hamilton, 1957.
95 Rempel, Richard A. *Unionists Divided: Arthur Balfour, Joseph Chamberlain and the Unionist Free Traders*, David and Charles, 1972.

Index